NASREDDIN HODJA

Eponym for Wit and Wisdom

NASREDDIN HODJA
Eponym for Wit and Wisdom

Mustafa Özçelik

BLUE DOME

Published by Blue Dome Press
535 Fifth Avenue, Ste.601
NY, 10017-8019

www.bluedomepress.com

Library of Congress Cataloging-in-Publication Data Available

ISBN: 978-1-935295-11-2

Printed by
Çağlayan A.Ş., İzmir - Turkey

CONTENTS

PREFACE

Nasreddin Hodja, the witty sage, is a transnational character whose jokes are told in many countries. His smiling face is very familiar not only in his homeland Anatolia but in many different countries around the world.

Was Nasreddin Hodja a real person or just an imaginary character? According to the reliable sources provided in the appendix, he lived in Anatolia in the 13th century. His jokes suggest that he held the respected position of a judge, teacher, or preacher; one thing we surely know is that Nasreddin Hodja was a colorful figure.

Are all of the jokes told about him authentic anecdotes from Nasreddin Hodja's life? As Said Nursi puts it, "Fame is a despot; it ascribes the property of others to the famous. Of the witticisms attributed to the famous Nasreddin Hodja, only its *zakah*, that is, one fortieth, can belong to him."[1] This study discusses essential characteristics and authenticity of his jokes and emphasize that the main purpose of Nasreddin Hodja's humorous stories was not amusement. He knew how to use humor to make people think. Nasreddin Hodja tried to draw attention to certain facts of the human condition through the use of humor. However, it is important to note that he did not intend to mock or humiliate any individual or groups in his stories.

Even though eight centuries have passed, Nasreddin Hodja's jokes still survive, for they were not only relevant to the thirteenth century. This book aims to provide a realistic portrait of this Anatolian sage based on his jokes and, most importantly, to shed light on his life and works.

---

1 Nursi, S., *Gleams of Truth*, Tughra Books, New Jersey: 2010.

CHAPTER ONE

The Era and Environment in Which Nasreddin Hodja Lived

"...The time period Nasreddin Hodja lived in coincides with the decline period of the Anatolian Seljuk Empire. A number of important events such as the Babai uprising, the Mongol invasion of Anatolia, the Seljuk princes' (*shahzadas*) fight over the crown, and the occupation of Anatolia by the Karamanid Dynasty took place in this period..."

Dr. Kenan Çağan

THE ERA AND ENVIRONMENT IN
WHICH NASREDDIN HODJA LIVED

A. THE CHARACTERISTICS OF THE ERA

What century did Nasreddin Hodja live in? There are two different approaches to this question and as a result two different answers. According to the first approach, he lived during the period in which Sultan Bayezid II ruled. It is possible to find information in some of the documents on Nasreddin and in some old periodicals on religion,[1] which supports this possibility. Evliya Çelebi is among the proponents of this opinion. There are also authors from the Republican era who agree with this view as well as some Western authors as well.[2]

This argument has been proven wrong today. For we have many stories informing us that he lived in during the rule of the Seljuk Emperor Alaeddin I: a note on Nasreddin's gravestone in 1393 left by of one of the soldiers of Sultan Bayezid I, Mehmed, nine years before the Mongol invasion of Ankara under the command of Timur (Tamerlane) indicates that he lived between 1208 and 1284. The *French Encyclopedia* too confirms that Nasreddin cannot be the contemporary of Timur.[3]

---

[1] Lamii Çelebi, *Letâif Mecmuası*.
[2] For example, Kantemir, Diez, Goethe, and Hammer are proponents of this view. But they base their argument on Evliya Çelebi's work, *Seyahatname* (The Book of Travels). For a comprehensive discussion on this, see İbrahim Hakkı Konyalı, "Nasreddin Hoca," *Yedi İklim* dergisi (Journal of *Yedi İklim*), ibid., page.169.
[3] Şükrü Kurgan, *Nasreddin Hoca*, p. 16.

Also, considering the recent studies on this issue, the more convincing argument is that Nasreddin Hodja lived in the Seljuk period and not during Ottoman rule. According to the *Mufti* of Sivrihisar, Hasan Efendi, Şemsettin Sami,[4] Mehmet Tahir from Bursa,[5] Fuat Köprülü,[6] İsmail Hami Danişmend,[7] İbrahim Hakkı Konyalı,[8] and non-Turkish researchers, Nasreddin Hodja lived during Seljuk rule in the 13th century.[9] During this period, sultans İzzeddin Keykavus I (1211-1219), Alaeddin Keykubat (1219-1237), Giyaseddin Keyhusrev II (1237-1246), İzzeddin Keykavus II (1246-1257), Rükneddin Kılıçarslan (1256-1257), Alaeddin Keykubad II (1249-1254), Giyaseddin Keyhusrev III (1266-1281), and Alaeddin Keykubad III (1297-1277) ruled.[10]

The Anatolian Seljuk Empire was in a decline period which would end with the collapse of this state. Only the rule of Sultan Alaeddin Keykubad I can be depicted as the heyday of this period. Nasreddin Hodja was a youngster during this highpoint which ends with the death of Alaeddin Keykubad I.

Important Historical Events of the Period

The unity of the Seljuk state came to an end following the Mongol invasion. The Mongol troops demolished and burnt everything they came across in Anatolia. Finally, the Seljuk army was routed after the Kösedağ War in 1243. The Seljuk Empire turned to an im-

---

[4] Şemsettin Sami (1850–1904) is an author from the Tanzimat period. He wrote extensively about Nasreddin Hodja in his book, *Kamus'ul'âlâm*.

[5] Bursalı Mehmet Tahir (1861–1924) is an author of biographies who wrote about Nasreddin Hodja.

[6] M. Fuat Köprülü (1890–1966) is a scholar and literary historian who extensively studied Nasreddin Hodja.

[7] İsmail Hami Danişmend (1899–1967), historian.

[8] İbrahim Hakkı Konyalı (1894–1984) is a researcher who conducted comprehensive research on Nasreddin Hodja.

[9] Eflatun Cem Güney, *Nasreddin Hoca Fıkraları* (Jokes of Hodja Nasreddin), p. 209.

[10] *Türk Ansiklopedisi* (Turkish Encyclopedia) vol.1, p. 138.

potent dynasty under Mongol rule. Soon after that, the Seljuk dynasty collapsed altogether.

A number of dynasties in Anatolia emerged following the collapse of the Anatolian Seljuk Empire. The people of Anatolia had to provide food to the Turkmens who fled the Mongol invasion to Erzurum, Erzincan and Sivas. In addition, the Anatolians provided the food supply of the soldiers hired from Egypt and Syria by the Seljuk sultans. It was a time of chaos and quite a number of uprisings emerged. The rulers of the dynasties cared for their own interests, and the people had to pay for the cost. Bribery, corruption and illegal activities were abundant. In line with this, the lack of order in the state led the princes to a fight against one another for power. The Karamanid dynasty, benefiting from the chaos, occupied Konya, the capital city of the Seljuk state.

Meanwhile, the Crusades added to the turbulence in Anatolia. The last four crusades took place during the lifetime of Nasreddin Hodja. Poverty was such a serious problem at the time that "some people had to eat the flesh of dead animals during the famine of 1299."[11] The social and political turmoil had reached its peak.[12] Many references to the hardships of that period are found in Hodja's jokes.

Nasreddin Hodja (1208-1284) was the contemporary of Jalaladdin Rumi (1207-1273),[13] Hacı Bektaş-ı Veli (1208?-1271),[14] Yunus Emre (1241-1321?),[15] Sheikh Edebali (death 1325),[16] and Sey-

---

11 Şükrü Kurgan, ibid., p. 18.

12 Şükrü Kurgan, Nasreddin Hoca Fıkralarında Türk Halk Yaşayışının İzleri, *Türk Dili Dergisi* (Journal of Turkish Language) issue 207, p. 844.

13 Jalaladdin Rumi is a great Sufi master and poet who lived in the 13th century.

14 Hacı Bektaş-ı Veli was a Sufi scholar in the 12th century whose most famous work is titled *Makalat*.

15 Yunus Emre, a spiritual leader who was born in Eskişehir, was a Sufi poet in the 13th century.

16 Şeyh Edebali (either Ede Balı or Edeb Ali), who died in 1325, was the father in law of Osman Bey, the founder of the Ottoman State.

yad Hamza (13th century).[17] In such a chaotic time period, Nasreddin Hodja shared the mission of the contemporary Sufis.

While the Sufis of the time endeavored to keep the rulers focused on their duties with religious and moral teachings, Nasreddin Hodja fulfilled the same message through his witty and humorous jokes full of wisdom and lessons which helped such a chaotic period to be overcome with the least amount of damage to the social memory. His jokes functioned as a source of optimism for people. He promoted good behavior among people while discouraging bad attitudes and deeds. As İbrahim Hakkı Konyalı put it: "His jokes, fraught with wisdom and lessons, appeared as a streak of lightning spreading hope and joy for the desperate souls in the period of decline and collapse."[18]

B. THE ENVIRONMENT IN WHICH HE LIVED

Born in Hortu, a village in Sivrihisar, Nasreddin Hodja lived in Hortu, Sivrihisar, Konya and Akşehir. He traveled to villages and towns in this region. It is evident from some of his jokes that he also traveled to other cities in Anatolia such as Bursa, Afyon and Kayseri. It can also be inferred from his jokes that he may have traveled to Kashgar, Turfan, Bukhara, and Samarkand.[19] In fact, although such an interpretation may lead us to conclude that he was originally from Turkistan and moved to Anatolia (Sivrihisar) due to the Mongol invasion, other evidence disproves this assumption.

---

[17] Seyyad Hamza was a Sufi minstrel in the 13th century. He wrote the first poems in Turkish prior to Yunus Emre.

[18] İbrahim Hakkı Konyalı, Nasreddin Hoca, *Yedi İklim* dergisi ibid., p. 169.

[19] The proponent of this argument, Şaban Abak, narrates the following story: [the Sultan of East Turkistan] calls the Hodja to his presence. "Hodja, you've travelled to lots of places in our country, and met our citizens. What is the most joyful day of our people? The Hodja responds: The happiest day of the people, as far as I am concerned, is the day you, the Majesty, will set out for Heaven." See Şaban Abak, ibid., p.17.

CHAPTER TWO

The Life of Nasreddin Hodja

"...Born in 1208, Nasreddin Hodja passed away in 1284 when he was 76. His place of birth is the Hortu village in Sivrihisar, Eskişehir..."

Şükrü Kurgan

THE LIFE OF NASREDDIN HODJA

A. PLACE OF BIRTH

There remained a cradle in Sivrihisar.

And a grave in Akşehir.

They become relatives

Akşehir and Sivrihisar

Arif Nihat Asya

Accccording to most researchers, Nasreddin Hodja was born in the Hortu village in Sivrihisar, Eskişehir, in the early 13th century (605 in the Islamic calender, and 1208 in the Gregorian calendar).[20] Some researchers from Akşehir also support this argument.[21]

There is a tomb in Azerbaijan that is also supposed to belong to Nasreddin Hodja.[22] However, the archives that provide information about Nasreddin's personality (e.g. law records, *Mecmua-i Maarif* –Journal of Education, *Saltukname*, etc.), archeological remains (the gravestone of his daughter was found in Sivrihisar, etc.), and the research of both Turkish and foreign scholars (Fuat Köprülü, Pertev Naili Boratav[23]), show that he was born in Hortu, now named after Nasreddin Hodja. Later on Hodja moved to

---

[20] Hortu Village became a municipality on 18 April 1999, and was named Nasreddin Hodja Municipality. It is located between Eskişehir and Ankara, 4 km from the highway.

[21] Kemal Uzun, *Nasreddin Hoca Araştırması*, p. 12 (The following is from that book: "Hodja Nasreddin was born in Hortu village in Sivrihisar, Eskişehir in 1208.")

[22] Kemal Uzun, ibid., p. 17.

[23] Pertev Naili Boratav (1907–1998) was a researcher of contemporary folk literature.

Konya and then to Akşehir[24] and lived in this town until he passed away.

B. FAMILY

Nasreddin's father, Abdullah Efendi, was the imam (prayer leader) of the Hortu village, and his mother, Sıdıka Hanım, was a native of the village. It was inferred from one of his jokes that he had a brother one year older than him.[25] After he moved to Akşehir, he got married and had children. According to the records, he had two wives, one of whom was from Sivrihisar and the other was from Akşehir. He had two daughters and a son.

C. EARLY EDUCATION

Nasreddin Hodja's first teacher was his father. His father taught him how to read and write and the basic pillars of Islam. Most likely, his father was a teacher at a *madrasa* (a traditional Islamic school). Nasreddin also learned Arabic and Persian. He memorized the Quran at a very early age, and his training included Islamic jurisprudence and theology as well.

He received the rest of his education from a few *madrasa*s in Sivrihisar. According to another account, his whole family had to move from Hortu to Sivrihisar due to famine. He moved back to Hortu following his father's death, and became the prayer leader and preacher there. He sometimes worked in Sivrihisar too.

It can be inferred from his jokes and other sources that the Hodja was a very energetic person. For this reason, he did not restrict himself to the mosque and *madrasa*, and chose to be with

---

[24] Mehmet Önder, Nasreddin Hoca Gerçeği, Minyatürlerle Nasreddin Hoca, p.7.

[25] The joke is as follows: When the Hodja was a child, they asked him, "Who is older? Your sibling or you?" Tittle Nasreddin opened his eyes wide. After calculating something in his mind, he said, "Last year my mom told me my brother was older than me. Based on this calculation, you could guess my age. I am now a year older. Now I am the same age as my brother. (See *Nasreddin Hoca ile Çocuklar*, Duhter Uçman p. 16–17.

people all the time and was interested in their problems. In this respect, it can be said that the realities of life along with his tendency to observe things became an integral part of his training. Yet Nasreddin was not satisfied with his formal education in Hortu and Sivrihisar, and chose to seek more knowledge. Owing to his desire for knowledge, he set off on a journey to the outside world, leaving behind his small village. The names of the different places mentioned in his jokes indicate that he went to other places before he reached Konya and Akşehir, and he had the opportunity to get to know many people. He seems to have sought scholars to learn more on his journeys. According to one author, Nasreddin travelled all around Central Asia following the route of the Mongols after the Karamanid occupation of Konya.[26]

D. DEPARTURE FROM SIVRIHISAR

The *madrasa*s in Konya and Akşehir were quite accomplished at the time. Konya and Akşehir used to be attractive places to visit for a lot of scholars, Sufis, travelers, and merchants. Thus, the *madrasa*s of Konya were always full of students and the dervish lodges were overflowing.

The ruling class as well as the notables of the city were involved with those institutions. The gates of the palaces and mansions were always open to scholars and Sufis. Konya, especially, as the capital city of the Seljuk Empire, also served as the cultural and educational capital. Sultan Alaeddin Keykubad I (1280-1237), who ruled at the time, was known for his respect for scholars in addition to his righteous rule.

Nasreddin Hodja had heard about the lively scholarly environment in those places. He most likely set out for Konya in 1233-1234 when he was in his early twenties leaving behind Mehmet (also known as Cılız Mehmet) as his successor for his position at the

---

26 Şaban Abak, *Bir Alperen Olarak Nasreddin Hoca*, *Yedi İklim* N. Hoca Special issue p. 13.

mosque.[27] After being educated in Konya, he returned to Sivrihisar. After a while, he continued his education in Akşehir in 1237 upon the invitation of his teacher and Tuğrul Efendi.

The following anecdote describes his trips to Konya and Akşehir. The castle warden of Sivrihisar, Alişar Bey asked Hodja what could be done to improve the city:

Nasreddin Hodja: "Our city will thrive with the presence of educated people. You can go to Konya and invite one of the prominent scholars here."

- Alişar Bey, spent 20 days convincing an intellectual to come to Sivrihisar, and he returned with Tuğrul Efendi.

- Tuğrul Efendi, who delivered speeches everyday, was able to impress the residents of Sivrihisar, including Nasreddin Hodja.

After a while, Tuğrul Efendi started to listen to Nasreddin Hodja's sermons. Discovering Nasreddin's talent and wit, he persuaded him to go to Akşehir and Konya to add to his knowledge and experience. Nasreddin decided to go to Akşehir and disclosed his decision to his family, friends and Tuğrul Efendi.

The Mongol influence was increasing in Anatolia during that period. A total state of unrest was prevalent throughout the region. Seeing that Nasreddin kept postponing his travel to Akşehir, Tuğrul Efendi told him, "Scholars should be guides for people. You will come across people longing for a cure for their moral shortcomings. You will place courage in them, and you will be cheerful even though you have problems of your own. That's the characteristic of a guide." Upon hearing Tuğrul Efendi's advice, he made his mind up quickly and set out for Akşehir.

He had to say goodbye to the place where he had lived for so long (Sivrihisar). All the people who loved him came to see him off on the day of his departure. His absence added to the sadness in the

---

[27] M. Fuat Köprülü, Nasreddin Hoca, p. 22, Kemal Uzun, Nasreddin Hoca Araştırması, p. 12 Şükrü Kurgan suggests that the Hodja's visit to Konya and his training in that city is a false account. According to Kurgan, the Hodja went to Akşehir instead of Konya. See Şükrü Kurgan, ibid., p. 17.

village during an era of hardship. When he mounted on his donkey, Alişar Bey told him in a sad voice, "Nasreddin Hodja! I knew that it was part of your plan. You made me find the person who would replace you first so that you could leave us. Don't think that I did not get it!"

Hodja pulled his donkey's headstall up to stop it. He swiftly turned around and sat on the donkey facing the backward and uttered the following: "Alişar Bey! Believe me, you are mistaken! Look, I am watching you! I am so sorry to leave you all behind."

Seeing Nasreddin sitting on his donkey facing the crowd, people could not help laughing. Nasreddin Hodja had fulfilled his task, and he set off for Akşehir on a Friday morning in the spring of 1237.

Nasreddin went to Emirdağ and then to Afyon where he met his former classmate Kul Ahmet. He rested at the Afyon-Gazlıgöl thermal springs, stopped by Boldavin, and finally reached Akşehir.

The residents of Akşehir were expecting Nasreddin Hodja warmly welcomed him. Shortly after, he went to the village of Maarif to visit Seyyid Hacı İbrahim Sultan only to hear that he had gone on a pilgrimage to Mecca. Then Nasreddin had to return to Akşehir where he started to lead the prayer and preach until his teacher İbrahim Sultan came back from the pilgrimage. His wife Atike (Hanım), his daughter Fatma, and his three nephews moved to Akşehir to live with him.[28]

Nasreddin Hodja added to his knowledge and experience by taking courses with other scholars and intellectuals in the region. Some commentators maintained that he might have pledged allegiance to Rumi and even might have met him based on the evidence that one of his teachers, Seyit Mahmud Hayrani, was a follower of Rumi.[29] The authenticity of this account is reinforced by the fact that Nasreddin also travelled to Konya and was educated by

---

[28] Kemal Uzun, ibid., p. 33.
[29] Yavuz Donat, *Sabah Daily Newspaper* 4. 5. 2004.

prominent scholars such as Hoca Fakih and Sadrettin Konevi. It was also claimed that he served as an advisor to the Anatolian Seljuk Sultan, Alaeddin Keykubat II, during his stay in Konya.[30]

Nasreddin Hodja, having completed his education in Konya, became a teacher at a *madrasa*. Haci Bektaş-ı Veli advised him to live in Akşehir since his Sheikh and teacher Hayrani also lived there. Nasreddin Hodja's house in Akşehir was a gift from Seyyid İbrahim Sultan, one of his teachers, İbrahim for he could not afford to buy one for himself due to the recession in the country and his poor economic situation.[31]

Nasreddin continued his scholarly work in Akşehir from then on. He taught at a *madrasa* while he also serving as a prayer leader, preacher, and judge. He spent a considerable portion of his life there.

E. MARRIAGE

It is evident from his jokes that Nasreddin Hodja was married several times. His first marriage took place after he moved to Akşehir. His first wife was an unattractive widow, who passed away shortly after they were married. After his first wife's death, he remarried.

Nasreddin and his wife had a daughter named Fatma. When Fatma got married, she moved to Sivrihisar. Her gravestone was found in Sivrihisar in 727 (Islamic calendar) which proves this account. According to the inscription on her gravestone, Fatma Hanım passed away in Sivrihisar in February 1326. This gravestone is on display in the Akşehir Museum. Fatma Hanım had a son named Celaleddin, who was a judge in Sivrihisar. Celaleddin's son, a great scholar, Hızır Bey was the first judge in Istanbul.[32] Hızır Bey's sons worked as prayer leaders in Sivrihisar and

---

[30] *Ibid.*
[31] Kemal Uzun, ibid., p. 15.
[32] *Yeni Türk Ansiklopedisi* vol.7 p. 2600.

Akşehir,[33] which illustrates that Nasreddin and his family continued to have a relationship with Sivrihisar even after they moved to Akşehir.

According to another account of Fatma Hanım, Nasreddin, before moving to Akşehir after completing his education in Konya, went back to the Hortu village in Sivrihisar and got married to Atike Hanım. Fatma Hanım was Atike Hanım's daughter.[34]

Which is the true story about Fatma Hanım? This is still undetermined. Nevertheless, regardless of the dispute over which one of these accounts accurately reflects the reality, it is certain that Nasreddin Hodja is from Sivrihisar,[35] which is supported by both of the accounts mentioned above.

Nasreddin Hodja and his second wife had another daughter named Dürr-i Melek Hatun. There is no information regarding her date of birth. Her gravestone is also is located in Nasreddin Hodja Cemetery in Akşehir. Nasreddin also had a son named Ömer or Şeyh Ömer, whose gravestone is also in the Sivrihisar Cemetery.[36] This also reinforces that Nasreddin is from Sivrihisar.

F. PROFESSIONAL LIFE

Based on the information found in his jokes, Nasreddin Hodja is thought to have worked as a prayer leader, preacher, muezzin (a man who calls the Muslims to prayer), intern prayer leader (*cer hocası*), clerk, teacher, judge, and consultant in court.[37]

---

[33] Kemal Uzun, ibid., p. 14.

[34] Kemal Uzun, ibid., p. 12.

[35] Fatma Hanım is from the Hodja's first marriage, and she went to Sivrihisar when she got married. Kemal Uzun also supports this argument. See Nasreddin Hoca Araştırması, p. 13.

[36] Hürriyetim online daily, 23. 7. 2003. The mayor of Sivrihisar, Fikret Aslan's, statement on the news "Nasreddin Hoca Paylasilamiyor".

[37] The title Hodja (*hace*) proves this as this word means "sir, master, teacher, head of the family, clerk, merchant and elderly" in all Turkic dialects. However, one should bear in mind that the meaning of the word has changed within time. See *Türk Dili ve Edebiyatı Ansiklopedisi* vol. 3 p. 443

He began his judiciary career as an intern judge and worked as a judge in Konya and Akşehir. Some commentators state that Nasreddin wanted to become a judge first, but seeing as some judges were receiving bribes he changed his mind. In addition, these commentators state that Nasreddin's Sufi worldview did not allow him to pursue a career as a judge.[38] According to another account, he worked as a judge until he moved to Akşehir. The characters who are judges and references to decrees in his jokes reinforce the argument that he was a judge.

Nasreddin Hodja also worked as a prayer leader and preacher in his village, Sivrihisar, and Akşehir. The first mosque he worked at in Akşehir was a small neighborhood mosque called *Kocakapı* (*İkikapı*) Mosque. He led the prayer and also preached in the neighboring villages and cities from time to time.

Nasreddin devoted most of his time to teaching at the *madrasas* and it is said that there used to be a *madrasa* in Akşehir named after Nasreddin Hodja. Even though this has not been proven yet, it is certain that he taught at different *madrasas* in Anatolia.

Besides working as a teacher and preacher, his jokes disclose that Nasreddin also worked as a tailor's apprentice, farmer, a grocer, and sold thread, olives, and eggs. He is even said to have worked as a physician in the rural areas, which shows that he was considered as one of the common people. In addition, the dire economic conditions of that time led him to work in various jobs. It can also be inferred from his jokes that he was unemployed at times due to the recession. When looking at his life as a whole, it can be determined that Nasreddin Hodja did not lead a prosperous life. He went through financial straits and was heavily in debt at times.[39]

Yet other accounts inform us that he was a well-to-do person. Evidence for this includes the foundation *madrasa* founded by him

---

[38] Âlim Yıldız ibid., p. 103.

[39] M. Sabri Koz, N. Hoca Bu Yollarda Neler Gördü? *İsfalt/Yol Kültürü Dergisi* July 1998 p. 65.

which İbrahim Hakkı Konyalı discusses in one of his articles. Even though this information can be verified and Nasreddin Hodja was rich at some point in his life, the largely accepted belief is that he did not have a very prosperous life. Taking the bad economic conditions of the time into account, it is impossible to claim that he was quite.[40] As Abdülbaki Gölpınarlı notes, "Nasreddin Hodja was not a man who enjoyed himself at harems and palaces with housemaids and eunuchs."[41]

G. APPEARANCE AND PERSONALITY

Based on books and lithographs written on Nasreddin Hodja, the following accuratedly describes his appearance and dress as an adult: "Nasreddin Hodja was neither too short nor too tall. He was a cheerful guy with a saintly face. He wore the same kind of clothes as the other men from the intellectual class did. His clothing consists of a cap and turban, a robe, a loose collarless shirt, baggy trousers with a belt, slippers, socks, a cotton handkerchief, and shoes. He also had a mustache and a beard as a sign of his piety.[42]

The following is another description of Nasreddin Hodja based on the miniatures (a type of art) which depict him: "Nasreddin Hodja was a man of religion who lived and dressed like other people in his community. He had a round face with a longish nose and slanting eyes which went well with his sizable turban, neat mustache, and long gray beard. He was neither tall nor short, and neither overweight nor skinny. Agile and strong, he always smiled while sitting on his donkey. The flaps of his robe fluttered about when he was in the Sultan Mountains and his short leather boots were a token of the days when he was a judge."[43]

---

[40] İ. Hakkı Konyalı, *Akşehir, Nasreddin Hoca'nın Şehri* p. 462.

[41] Abdülbaki Gölpınarlı, *Nasreddin Hoca*.

[42] Kemal Uzun, ibid., p. 18.

[43] Cited by Saim Sakaoğlu, Fıkra Tiplerinin Değişmesi, Folklor ve Etnografya Araştırmaları p. 445 (This depiction was featured by the deputy mayor of Akşehir, Mustafa Yıldırımer.)

H. Death and Tomb

Nasreddin Hodja passed away at age 76 in Akşehir in 1284 (Gregorian calendar). He was buried in a dome-shaped tomb surrounded by six columns in the oldest Seljuk cemetery in Akşehir. All four sides of Nasreddin Hodja's first tomb were open, and an unlocked padlock hung on the gate facing the direction of Mecca.

According to İbrahim Hakkı Konyalı, his tomb was neglected until the residents of Akşehir decided to take care of it in 1878. Finally, upon the initiative of the governor of Konya, Faik Bey, and the district governor of Akşehir, Mustafa Şükrü Bey, the tomb of Nasreddin Hodja was restored during the rule of the Sultan Abdulhamid II in 1905 Akşehir and a four-line epitaph was added on it.[44] The Akşehir municipality has been responsible for the regular maintenance of the tomb from then on.

Quite a few authors of travel books as well as the residents of Akşehir have provided information about Nasreddin Hodja's tomb. The following passage describes the physical condition of his tomb:

Even though it was an open-air tomb, it, nevertheless, had a huge door. A dome and walls were built, and it was surrounded by a fence later on by the initiative of the notables of the region. Reminiscent of a water-tank with a fountain that is usually found in mosques, the architecture of the tomb is a monument of peculiarity. There is a turban over the sarcophagus placed over the grave of the eminent Hodja, which seemed to be equal to the one third of the sarcophagus. The following statement was articulately inscribed on a piece of stone erected in front of the sarcophagus: "This is the tomb of the deceased. May he be forgiven by God. Recite a prayer for Nasreddin Hodja."[45]

---

[44] İ. Hakkı Konyalı, *Akşehir, Nasreddin Hoca'nın Şehri* p. 463

[45] Cited by Alpay Kabacalı from Yâd-ı Mâzi by Bereketzâde İsmail Hakkı. *Bütün Yönleriyle Nasreddin Hoca* p. 80-81

I. NASREDDIN HODJA IN ANECDOTES

"No matter how important a historical figure Nasreddin Hodja is, he is represented in the real sense in the unique, glowing face that centuries presented to him."

Prof. Dr. M. Fuad Köprülü

Nasreddin Hodja, like many other eminent individuals, has, in addition to his actual personality and life story, a mythical personality and life. The made-up story of Nasreddin Hodja was born out of people's love for him. He was embraced by the people from every region in Anatolia. These people depicted him as being from their region and portrayed him with the kind of personality they liked most. As a result, , there are multiple variations of his personality and life story which has led to skepticism as to whether or not he existed at all. The following sentence sums up this issue: "Nasreddin Hodja's legendary folkloric figure overshadowed his historical figure after a while."[46]

According to the legends, the speculations about his birth place not only took place in Sivrihisar and Akşehir but also in other places ranging from the Balkans to Central Asia. Therefore, in can be concluded that Nasreddin Hodja was well known in many different areas.

An examination of the anecdotes created by people shows the people's perspective of Nasreddin Hodja. Most of the time, such an analysis shows a very different Hodja, especially in terms of the characteristics of the era in which he lived. One such anecdote describes the friendship between Nasreddin Hodja and Mansur al-Hallaj and Seyyid Nesimi. What makes this anecdote interesting is that a particular piece of information is given to emphasize the Hodja's humorous characteristic.

---

[46] Şükrü Kurgan, ibid., p. 5.

Nasreddin Hodja, Seyyid Nesimi[47] and Mansur al-Hallaj[48] were friends according to this anecdote. All of them were students of Seyyid Hayrani at the Akşehir *madrasa*. All the other *mollas* (students in a *madrasa*) loved them and listened to Nasreddin's jokes, Nesimi's poems and Mansur's stories whenever they gathered on the porch.

One day, Hayrani had to visit his village and entrusted his beloved lamb to Nasreddin Hodja, Nesimi and Mansur. They decided to take a walk in the fields with the lamb. When they became hungry, they decided to eat the lamb. Mansur slaughtered the lamb and Nesimi was tasked with removing its skin. They asked Nasreddin Hodja to help them. He responded, "Seyyid Hayrani is a blessed person, so I cannot touch his lamb. Yet I won't be able to resist eating it if you cook it." After cooking it, they ate the entire lamb.

Seyyid Hayrani was angry with them when he returned and found out what had happened to his lamb. He asked who slaughtered his lamb. Mansur admitted that he had done it. Nesimi admitted that he skinned the lamb. Seyyid Hayrani turned to Nasreddin Hodja to find out what role he had played in this. Nasreddin replied, "I laughed at what they did and ate the lamb." Seyyid Hayrani looked at them again and replied, "Mansur, one day they will slaughter you like this; Nesimi, they will skin you like you skinned

---

47 Seyyid Nesimi was the first prominent poet and thinker in Azeri-Turkish literature. Interested in poetry and Sufism, he pledged allegiance to Mansur al-Hallaj in his youth. A follower of Hurufism (a mystical kabbalistic Sufi doctrine), he was killed by excoriation in Halep. See *Türk Dili ve Edebiyatı Ansiklopedisi* vol. 7 p. 20–21 for more information on this.

48 Mansur al-Hallaj was one of the great Sufis. He was the follower of Cüneydî Bağdadî. He played a significant role in spreading Islam to Isfahan, Horasan and the Kum region. Later, he was imprisoned for saying, "I am God" and sentenced to capital punishment. First, he was whipped and then his hands, feet and head were cut off. His body was hung from scaffolding. Finally, he was burnt and his ashes were thrown into the Tigris river. See for further information, see *Türk Dili ve Edebiyatı Ansiklopedisi* vol. 4 p. 74–75.

my lamb; and Nasreddin, they will laugh at you till the end of this world. You asked for this and so is God's will."[49]

People from Akşehir have a saying: "No wedding is complete without guests, and no gathering is complete without Nasreddin Hodja." Nasreddin was the most respected guest at every gathering. He would show up regardless of whether he was invited. Even if he could not make it to an event, his place would be kept vacant. Unfortunately, on many occasions he did not have a chance to eat the food served since he was busy answering questions.

His friends in the neighborhood where he grew up were jealous of him even though they loved him a lot because as a child Nasreddin always spoiled his friends' plans against him. The youth as well as the elderly loved him. He had good relations with his neighbors. He never missed an opportunity to give lessons to his lazy, unskilled, and hypocritical neighbors and those who tended to exploit the feelings of others.

The Anatolian people suffered a lot when Timur invaded, but this occupation took place long after Nasreddin Hodja passed away. Thus, the Timur figure in the anecdotes represents all authority figures and is a symbol of oppression. Therefore, those jokes attributed to Nasreddin Hodja play an important role in the psychological relief of the masses.

M. Fuat Köprülü describes Nasreddin Hodja's place in people's hearts: "The people of Akşehir venerate Nasreddin Hodja and believe in his holiness. Some superstitions emerged as a result of this intensive love for him. For instance, people visit his tomb before every wedding ceremony and invite him along with his *molla* (students) to their wedding. Otherwise, it is believed that the newlywed couple will not get along well with each other. Similarly, if a person who sees his tomb does not laugh, he or she is doomed to a catastrophic incident. It is also believed that if a person with a cer-

---

[49] *Yurt Ansiklopedisi*, Konya Kültürü, Yöresel Halk Edebiyatı Bölümü issue. 5234, Nezihe Araz, Anadolu Erenleri p. 347–348.

tain type of impaired vision takes a piece of soil from his tomb and wipes it on their eyes, their eyes will be healed."[50] The superstitious beliefs and anecdotes fabricated about him illustrate the deep respect for Nasreddin Hodja regardless of whether those stories are true or not.

J. RELATIONSHIP WITH TIMUR[51]

In spite of the common acceptance that they were not contemporaries, there are a number of Nasreddin Hodja jokes about Timur. Those who argue that Nasreddin Hodja was the contemporary of Timur build their arguments on such jokes as well as similar ones, and claim that he lived during the rule of Sultan Bayezid I. Çaylak Tevfik Bey is one of the proponents of this view. In addition, in *the Book of Travels* Evliya Çelebi suggests that Nasreddin Hodja and Timur were contemporaries.

According to historical records, Nasreddin Hodja lived 120 years before Timur. The Ankara War (1402) took place between Timur and Sultan Bayezid I 120 years after Nasreddin's death. Later research has shown that these jokes which are attributed to Nasreddin were written by the renowned poet, Tacettin İbrahim bin Hızır Bey, whose pen name was Ahmedi. This poet, who wrote *İskendername*, was from Amasya. He wrote this work on the behalf of one of the princes of Sultan Bayezid I, Emir Süleyman. He also lived in Timur's palace for a while.[52]

Why did people to insert Timur into Nasreddin Hodja's jokes? Why did people create a relationship between them in the jokes? According to Nihat Sami Banarlı, even though Nasreddin Hodja

---

50 M. Fuat Köprülü, *Nasreddin Hoca* p. 23 (Veled Çelebi too reports of the existence of such beliefs). See *Letaif-i Hoca Nasreddin* p. 19.

51 Timur (1336-1405), or Tamerlane, is an Uzbek commander who imposed his rule over a vast territory – from the Mediterranean to Syberia. He occupied Anatolia and captured Ottoman Sultan Yıldırım Bayezid, dissolving the Ottoman army. He is one of the few historical figures who changed the direction of history. See *Türk Ansiklopedisi*, vol. 11 p. 4108.

52 İbrahim Hakkı Konyalı, "Nasreddin Hoca," *Yedi İklim* dergisi, ibid., p. 169.

lived in the 13th century, these recreated jokes have him meet Timur 116 years after his death to avenge oppression. Thus, Nasreddin Hodja lived for centuries and has become the infinite source of joy, the unbreakable needle, and the invincible warrior.[53]

Foreign scholars make similar comments on this. Edmund Saussey points out, "It is meaningful that the Turkish people completed this honest and kind-hearted man's portrait by positioning him against Timur. Nasreddin Hodja has become the national symbol that shows that the jovial courage together with peaceful perseverance could beat the recalcitrance, and feelings of power."[54]

K. OTHER NASREDDINS

The name Nasreddin or Nasuriddin was very common name at the time he lived. The prevalence of his name resulted in people confusing him with other Nasreddins who lived at that time. Besides, there was already confusion due to the fact that his legendary personality overshadowed his historical existence. In fact, quite a few people have exactly the same name or slight variations. Ahmet Baydar lists some of those names in one of his articles:

1. Nasıruddin Berkiyaruk, son of İzzeddin Kılıçarslan.
2. Nasuriddin Nasrullah b. Kuh Arslan, envoy of Sultan Keykavus II, who was sent to Baybars in 1261.
3. Nasuriddin Oğulmuş, who was sent to Keykavus II in 1261 by Baybars as an armorer.[55]
4. Nasıruddin Abdulcebbar, a Sufi man of literature who lived during the rule of Sultan Gıyasettin II.
5. Nasuriddin Ali, a currency controller of the currency during the rule of Sultan Alaeddin.[56]

---

53 Nihat Sami Banarlı, *Resimli Türk Edebiyatı* vol. 1, p. 304.
54 Edmond Saussey (Cited by Petev Naili Boratav), *Folklor ve Edebiyat 2*. p.303.
55 Silahtar (Silahdar): An armorer who is responsible for the weapons of the pashas and viziers.
56 Çâşni-gîr: A gourmet who checks the taste of the food in palaces, the chef.

6. Nasuriddin Osman, prayer leader in a neighborhood called Seyfeddin Sungur in Malatya and a judge in Darende.

7. Nasuriddin Nusret İnanç, judge in Konya.

8. Nasuriddin Çelebi, a well-known rich person.[57]

In addition to those mentioned above, Nasuriddin, the son of Yavlak Arslan, one of the viziers of Sahip Ata, the sultan of Delhi in India; Nasuriddin Mahmud; and one of the viziers of Hulagu, Hodja Nasuriddin Tusi, were among the namesakes of Nasreddin Hodja.[58]

No matter how similar these names were to one another, current research has shown that there is only one Nasreddin Hodja, who was born in Sivrihisar and died in Akşehir. There remains some disputes over the authenticity of a small portion of the jokes.[59]

[57] Ahmet Baydar, Bilge Hoca, *Yedi İklim* dergisi, ibid., p. 168.

[58] Kemal, Uzun, ibid., p. 20.

[59] İ. Hakkı Konyalı, *Yedi İklim* dergisi, ibid., p. 171.

Chapter Three

Nasreddin Hodja in Turkish Literature

"Nasreddin Hodja's name has been mentioned in various written documents since the 15th century. The oldest of those books is *Saltukname*, written by Ebu'l Hayr-ı Rumi in 1480 upon the order of Cem Sultan."

Dr. Mustafa Duman

NASREDDIN HODJA IN TURKISH LITERATURE

A. *SALTUKNAME*

altukname is written in prose by Ebu'l Hayr-ı Rumi in 1480 upon the request of Cem Sultan (an Ottoman prince). The book tells the story of Sarı Saltuk, a heroic soldier. When Sultan Izzeddin Keykavus II, the son of Sultan Keyhusrev II asked for a piece of land to settle onwith his entourage following the Mongol invasion of Anatolia, the Byzantine Emperor allocated Dobruca in Romania to them. The first party of immigrants who moved to Dobruca included approximately 30 groups of Turkmen nomads. Sarı Saltuk was a veteran dervish and the chief of the first nomadic groups who moved to Dobruca.[60]

There are different accounts of him. The book *Velayetname*, for instance, describes Sarı Saltuk as a former shepherd, who became a saint (a friend of God) after being taught by Hacı Bektaş, and was sent to Dobruca as his teacher's deputy. He was also friends with the sheikh (religious master) of Nasreddin Hoca, and a prominent Sufi of the time, Seyyid Mahmud Hayrani.

In *Saltukname*, which is about the spread of Islam and the Turkification of Rumeila (the European part of the Ottoman Empire) through the persona of Sarı Saltuk, the jokes of Nasreddin Hodja were also mentioned.

Sarı Saltuk's visit to Nasreddin Hodja following his visit to Seyyid Mahmud Hayrani's grave was narrated in the book. This section is important since it reveals Nasreddin's relationship with Sivrihisar:

---

[60] *Türk Dili ve Edebiyatı Ansiklopedisi* vol. 7 p. 446–447.

"Sarı Saltuk left Konya for Akşehir, and visited the grave of Seyyid Mahmud Hayrani.

After paying his respects to Hayrani, Sarı Saltuk went to Nasreddin Hodja's home.

He knocked on the door. Nasreddin's wife appeared at the door and asked,

'Who are you?'

Saltuk answered back:

'I am Saltuk. Where is Nasreddin?'

Hodja's wife told him:

'he went to Sivrihisar and Karahisar.'

Saltuk said:

'Alas! I came to get some advice from him, but he is not here.'

Hodja's wife told him,

'If that is what you want, I can give you some advice. Take my advice if you like it.

Here is my advice for you: First, do not be friends with evil-doers and transgressors.

Do not trust such people with your property and yourself.

Do not reveal your secrets to them.

Ask for repentance from God all the time.

Whatever you ask for yourself, ask for for the same for your fellow believers.

Fear God and feel humble before His Messenger.

And acquire merits and good deeds for the Hereafter.

Stay away from mischievous people and do not commit mischievous behavior so that your heart does not get tarnished so that you could discover the hidden and mysterious and admire the Truth.'

Upon hearing this invaluable advice from Nasreddin's wife, Saltuk gave her 100 gold coins as a gift, and left.

It is said that Saltuk sent gifts to Nasreddin Hodja and his wife every year, and they would pray for Saltuk in return. One year, Saltuk did not send a gift, and Nasreddin and his wife did not pray for him. Then, Saltuk sent them gifts, and asked them,

'Is this how you treat your friends?'

Nasreddin Hodja responded,

'My friend, don't you know that you cannot keep a horse with an empty bag? This is a mistake according to men of wisdom.'"[61]

B. *Letaif*

The book titled *Letaif* by Lamii is another source with information on Nasreddin Hodja. This book includes three of Nasreddin Hodja's jokes. Those jokes also indicate that he is from Sivrihisar:

"A Karamanid scholar comes before Mevlana Sinan Pasha, who belonged to the same family as Nasreddin Hodja, who was among the notables of Sivrihisar. The pasha asked the scholar:

'Where are you from?'

The scholar replied,

'Pasha, I am from Karaman and Anatolia.'

Pasha continued in a teasing manner,

'The air and water of Karaman make people peaceful and its mountains and nature make them cheerful. So, how do you explain the disgrace and guilt cast upon them?

The scholar responded,

'There are two reasons for that. First, Karaman is very close to Sivrihisar, and the other reason is that Karaman is the graveyard of Nasreddin Hodja in Akşehir.'

Pasha found the scholar's answer very pleasing and praised him.[62]

C. *Seyahatname (The Book of Travels)* *of Evliya Çelebi*

The great voyager Evliya Çelebi stopped by Akşehir and visited Nasreddin Hodja's tomb. Evliya Çelebi describes this visit in the third

---

61 *Türk Edebiyatı* dergisi, Nasreddin Hoca Anıt issue p. 53. Also see Pertev Naili Boratav, Folklor ve Edebiyat 2, p. 306–307.

62 Lâmizâde Abdullah Çelebi, *Lâtifeler*, p. 43–44.

volume of *Seyahatname* along with an anecdote that is believed to have taken place between Nasreddin Hodja and Timur which led some researchers to think that Timur and Hodja were contemporaries. Since the authenticity of this argument has been discussed in the previous section, the chapter on Nasreddin Hodja in *Seyahatname* will be focused on here:

"He (Nasreddin Hodja) is from Akşehir. He lived during the rule of Sultan Murad Hüdavendigar and Sultan Bayezid I. He was a man of virtue and wisdom known to be a good believer, able to work miracles, and a moderate man following the straight path. He was the contemporary and a friend of Timur. Out of his respect and love for Nasreddin Hodja, Timur enjoyed conversing with him and did not destroy Akşehir. The jokes and advice of Nasreddin Hodja are used as proverbs in the language."[63]

Evliya Çelebi's notes from his visit

"A tomb located in the south of Akşehir township, surrounded by an iron fence draws the attention of all passers-by.

In this tomb rests the great religious scholar, a man of wit and intuition, the teller of those famous jokes, Nasreddin Hodja.

Nasreddin Hodja is a person known for his repartee and mature personality. Even Timur, the invader of Anatolia, refrained from plundering Akşehir out of his respect and sympathy for Nasreddin.

Several books note the following anecdote that took place between Timur and Hodja.

One day, Timur and Nasreddin went to a *hamam* (Turkish public bath), and while they were talking, Timur asked him a question: 'Nasreddin Hodja, you know I am a great sultan. How much do you think I would cost if I were a piece of property?'

---

[63] Cafer Erkılıç, *Evliya Çelebi*, p. 37.

Since Nasreddin is an honest man who does not refrain from expressing what he thinks, he replied, 'I would say you cost 40 silver coins.'

Upon hearing this unexpected answer, Timur got angry, 'Nasreddin, this bathrobe alone cost 40 coins. What do you say?'

Nasreddin Hodja replied without any hesitation,

'I would buy that bathrobe of yours for 40 coins. Otherwise, you are not even worth a penny.'

Hearing such an honest remark from Nasreddin Hodja pleased Timur and made him forget his initial anger. He appreciated Nasreddin's honesty and rewarded him for expressing what he really thought.

So, I stopped by Akşehir during my long journey in Anatolia. I could not leave Akşehir without visiting Nasreddin Hodja's tomb.

It was about midnight. I left the city for his tomb with one of my assistants. I could not help laughing when I suddenly thought of a couple of Nasreddin Hodja's jokes on the way to his tomb.

When we reached his tomb, I greeted him,

'Peace be upon you, Hodja!'

Of course, I did not expect a response to this greeting, yet that was not the case. I heard a voice saying, 'peace be upon you too, the great man!'

My horse stood up on its hind legs upon hearing the voice and hid inside the tomb. At that moment, a person appeared at the tomb's door,

'Sir, would you make a donation? May you go in peace.' After a short conversation with the owner of the mysterious voice, we were relieved to hear that he was the watchman at the tomb.

I pretended to be angry with what the watchman did in order to play with him, and said: 'Sir! I greeted the man resting in this tomb, not you, because you are not dead. Why did you respond to it?'

I wanted to conceal my astonishment by reproaching him. I did not want to prolong the conversation. We gave some money to him and left the tomb. Of course, we did not neglect to pray for Nasreddin Hodja while we were in his presence.

I could not help laughing at what happened at the tomb on our way back. Nasreddin Hodja keeps amusing people even while dead.[64]

D. *ÂSÂR-I PERÎŞÂN*

Mehmet Tevfik Bey compiled Nasreddin Hodja's jokes in three volumes. He provides the following information about Nasreddin Hodja. Nasreddin Hodja has such a good reputation that there is no one in the Turkic world who has not heard of him and who would not smile when his name is mentioned. Recently, his fame even reached Europe as some of his jokes have been translated into French.

The stories attributed to Nasreddin Hodja are, in essence, all about wisdom and truth presented in a humorous manner.

It is fair to say that he is a philosopher trained in the school of nature. He is buried in Akşehir, yet his name lives on in every city.

During the rule of Sultan Bayezid II, one of Hodja's children went to the gate of Asarfi to submit a petition in order to receive some livelihood from the foundations of the Sultan for being a family member of Nasreddin Hodja. He tied his horse to the ceremonial drum left in the public square. As the horse began dragging the drum, it was intimidated by the sound; as it tried to get away, the dragging drum made more noise and the horse was scared further. Coincidentally, the mules of the Surre Caravan (of royal gifts to the two sacred cities) which were passing there were also frightened by the noise of the drum. Thus, the people around became curious about the clamor. When they asked who tied the

---

[64] Evliya Çelebi, *Seyahatname [The Book of Travels]* vol. 3 p. 16-17 (Abbreviated).

horse to the drum, they found out that it was the petitioner who claimed to be one of the children of Nasreddin Hodja. They did not doubt who he was and did not ask any further questions to prove it. The man was given what he asked for.

Most of the interesting and witty jokes of Nasreddin Hodja, which circulate in the tongues of people have not been printed and recorded yet. A printed copy of the common jokes of Nasreddin Hodja was translated into French.

A lot of jokes attributed to Nasreddin Hodja that were not included in the book mentioned above were compiled with other jokes excerpted from the printed copy with meticulously chosen pictures added and locally published.[65]

E. *KÂMUS'UL A'LÂM*

There is an entry on Nasreddin Hodja in the encyclopedia *Kamusu'l Alam* written by Şemseddin Sami,[66] a renowned encyclopedist and lexicographer. The following is the information provided in that book:

> "Nasreddin (Hodja) was a refined man, although believed to be the contemporary of Hacı Bektaş-ı Veli, it is most likely that he lived long before, during the rule of the Seljuk Empire. Since lots of jokes have been attributed to him, Nasreddin Hodja has become the epitome of the humor tradition probably due to the lack of information on his life history. It is believed that the open-air tomb in Akşehir upon which hangs a huge lock belongs to him. Others narrate anecdotes about Timur and Nasreddin Hodja maintaining that they lived in the same time period."[67]

---

65 Mehmet Tevfik Bey, from *Âsâr-ı Perîşân* (Cited by M. Sabri Köz), *Yedi İklim* dergisi issue 138-139 p. 45.

66 Şemsettin Sami was a Tanzimat (Ottoman period of reform) poet whose work included novels, drama, dictionaries, encyclopedias and various translations.

67 Şemseddin Sami, *Kâmus'ul a'lâm* vol. 6.

CHAPTER FOUR

Nasreddin Hodja's Personality

"...Nasreddin Hodja, depicted as a comedian by some incompetent researchers, oblivious to our national and religious culture, was indeed a spiritual guide and a moralist..."

Dr. Mustafa Tatçı

NASREDDIN HODJA'S PERSONALITY

A. PERSONALITY

The following is an overall description of Nasreddin Hodja's personality based on his jokes and documents on his life history.

a) First of all, Nasreddin Hodja was knowledgable at both religious and non-religious sciences. He was taught by the greatest scholars of his time.

b) He was the man of the community. His life was not restricted to the *madrasa* and dervish lodges. Instead, he was a scholar who preferred to share his knowledge and experience with people from all walks of life.

c) Even when he was not directly involved in an incident, he was able to help with resolving conflicts and gave advice on various situations. His ability to observe things from a distance, his objectivity, and to pinpoint the source of problems enabled him to distinguish between right and wrong.

d) He was well respected by both the lay people and the administrative class. People always consulted with him on various issues. In this respect, he was a teacher, educator and a consultant.

e) He was respected and loved not only during his life time, but also in the centuries after his death for his ability to embellish his scholarly and didactic side with mellifluous language and a smiling face. This quality stems from his faith as well as from his personality.

f) He was known for his quick wit. Yet, it is misleading to depict him as "a funny guy" since the ability to make people laugh requires the ability to think deeply and to make people contemplate. Even though the first response one of his jokes is laughter, that laughter is usually followed by some thought.

g) Thinking was part and parcel of his life. He especially liked to think about issues such as life, death, predestination, and fortune. For instance, his 'pumpkin' joke is a perfect example of his love of thinking:

One day Nasreddin Hodja was working in his orchard. When he stopped for a break, he sat under a walnut tree and pondered.

"You Almighty God," he said, "it's your business, but why would you grow huge pumpkins on weak branches on the ground, and house little walnuts on a strong and mighty tree?" As he contemplated, a walnut fell from the tree right onto his head.

"Great God," he said, "now I understand why you did not find the pumpkins suitable for the tree. Do as you see it fit! It would have been a pumpkin if you had the same reasoning as me." This joke indicates how Nasreddin Hodja observed and contemplated on things around him and learned from them.

h) His attempt to entertain people would, by no means, turn into flattery or obsequiousness. For this reason, he is not seen as a comedian.

i) It is also crucial to note that his wit should not be confused with guile. For being cunning requires one to find illicit ways to overcome a difficulty whereas being witty gives one the ability to see the legitimate but indiscernible means to resolve an issue.

j) The seemingly naive and foolish statements in Nasreddin Hodja's jokes should not be misinterpreted. Nasreddin

Hodja usually criticized himself with such remarks; or, he uses such remarks to reveal a bitter truth. Yet he never fails to deliver his subtle point in the end.

k) Despite his prestigious status in society, it is hard to distinguish Nasreddin Hodja from an average man in his community in terms of his living standards. While fulfilling his primary tasks as a prayer leader, teacher and judge, he does not fail to be in close contact with the lay people. It is not surprising to see him go into the forest to cut trees like the others do. He does the shopping for his household. He trades like other people do. He is so industrious that he fixes his leaking roof and ploughs his farm.

l) Nasreddin Hodja emphasized religious duty to encourage people to do good deeds and to discourage them from doing the opposite. He describes the cures for social illnesses and problems by criticizing the root causes of these problems.

m) He was so gentle toward people that he never hurt them or looked down upon them. He tended to forgive people's mistakes.

n) He lived during a very chaotic era. His jokes became a source of joy for people who were struggling with the turbulence of the time. He taught people to overcome problems by not attaching too much importance to them. Despite the problems, he advised people to appreciate and be grateful for the life they were given and to seek ways to enjoy it. He tried to show people that it was possible to find some good in every bad situation.

o) Nasreddin Hodja was respectful to faith, ethics, the state, laws, and social norms but this did not deter him from criticizing the statesmen, bureaucrats, and religious authorities. He did not refrain from satirizing the corrupt judges, the religious figures who exploit people in the name of religion, the superficial scholars, and the oppressive administrators. His subtle use of satirical language did not create enemies for him, instead, the people he addressed in his jokes took him seriously.

p) He did not fail to criticize himself. Self-criticism requires a person to be mature, and Nasreddin Hodja exemplified such behavior.

r) He was by no means a visionary or escapist. On the contrary, he was a realist. He never exaggerated or dreamed about things.

s) He did not only carry the characteristics of his society, but also those of humanity. For this reason, he succeeded in becoming a character known both nationally and internationally.

t) In some jokes, Nasreddin Hodja is portrayed as someone who does not observe the essential religious practice like Ramadan fasting and the daily prayers. In fact, it is ironic to assume that he was not an observant, practicing Muslim since the most reliable information about him reveals that he was a sincere Muslim who observed his duties.

u) He did reflect the overall characteristics of Turkish Muslims, both as a believer and as an individual in his roles as a prayer leader, judge, merchant and farmer.

B. AS A SCHOLAR

Nasreddin Hodja's scholarship is noteworthy. His outstanding education started at an early age with his father. Then, he studied in *madrasas* in Sivrihisar and Konya. He was a teacher at a *madrasa*. He was lucky to be acquainted with the prominent scholars of his time and so he was part of a remarkable educational and scholarly environment.

While he was a scholar he was not pedantic; he did not show off his knowledge. He did not rely solely on books to find answers. Instead, he preferred to come up with innovative ways to interpret various situations in life using reason and judgement. In addition, he was critical of predominant educational methods. For instance, he did not approve of the education system in the *madrasas* which was based on memorization. The following joke is a striking example of his criticism of that matter.

One day, Nasreddin Hodja's neighbor asked him to write something to be used as an amulet for his sleepless child. Instead of doing that, he recommended that the neighbor place a thick book, which he taught at *madrasa* to his students, under the child's pillow. When the neighbor asked if it was a type of amulet, Nasreddin Hodja responded, "I don't know if it is an amulet or not, but I am pretty sure that it makes my students fall asleep in class whenever I read a passage from it."

At a time when individuals were not allowed to carry weapons, Nasreddin Hodja was caught with a sword. When the police (*subaşı*) asked him why he carried a sword, he explained, "I scrape off the mistakes of my students with this sword. That's why I keep it with me." When the police officer told him that a small jack-knife could do that, Nasreddin replied, "Even this sword is not big enough to scrape some mistakes off." Although probably he intended to smooth over the situation with this joke, it should be interpreted as severe criticism of the wrong methods and inconsistencies in the education system.

Nasreddin Hodja deemed it important that knowledge be based on truth and be able to be used practically. The following joke illustrates his stance on this issue. One day, three scholars came to Akşehir to talk to him. They asked, "Nasreddin Hodja, where is the center of the earth?" Pointing to his donkey which was next to them, he said, "It is under the right hind foot of my donkey." "How do you know?" one of the scholars asked. "If you do not believe me, go and measure it," Nasreddin Hodja replied. The second scholar asked, "How many stars are in the sky?" "There are as many stars as there are bristles on my donkey," he answered. The third one asked, "How many bristles are there in my beard?" "As many as the bristles on my donkey's tail," he replied. When the third person continued, "How can you prove it?" Nasreddin Hodja said, "If you do not believe me, we can begin plucking the bristles of your beard and the donkey's tail one by one to compare!"

What Nasreddin Hodja wanted to stress with this joke is that it is pointless for scholars to spend time and energy on unjustifiable and inconsequential details because there is usually no provable answer to such questions. Even though there is an answer, such knowledge is fruitless.

C. As a Sufi

Ali Günvar, a contemporary poet, shares his impressions of Nasreddin Hodja in one of his articles, "It is fair to say that Nasreddin Hodja is a saintly person who was able to make people think over the existing socio-policital issues through the use of humour within the Islamic norms during a time of abundant social crises purported by a recession, followed by the decline of the unitarian, monolithic and oppressive ideology of the state."[68]

Like the many other researchers who study the life and work of Nasreddin Hodja, Ali Günvar also refers to him as a"saint". Nasreddin Hodja was also depicted as a Sufi, a dervish, a deputy to the religious sheikhs, and a sheikh in other accounts. He is characterized as a saint in Bayburtlu Osman's book, which is cited in the section on sources on Nasreddin Hodja. This information resonates with how people think of Nasreddin. Accordingly, his jokes have mainly been interpreted from a Sufi perspective. For instance, Burhaneddin Çelebi (1814-1897), the grandson of Mawlana Jalaluddin Rumi, interpreted 121 of Nasreddin Hodja's jokes from a Sufi point of view.

---

[68] Ali Günvar, Bana Damdan Düşmüş Olan Bir Doktor Getirin, *Yedi İklim* Nasreddin Hoca Özel Sayısı, p. 10.

Sabri Tandoğan echoes Ali Günvar's thoughts on Nasreddin Hodja, "Nasreddin Hodja's jokes should not be seen simply as farce or as funny little stories. A Sufi-based reading of his jokes would reveal that humanity has a lot to learn from him."[69] Another scholar, İsmail Emre, born in 1900 in Adana, took the same approach to his study of Nasreddin Hodja's jokes. Emre sensed the spiritual wisdom of his jokes and interpreted them accordingly.[70] For Emre too, Nasreddin Hodja was a great Sufi, who infused the Sufi ethics in his jokes. The Sufi themes in his jokes function as a measure to distinguishe the authentic jokes from those attributed to him.[71]

Nasreddin Hodja is a scholarly man. Starting at a very early age, he received intensive religious education, memorized the Qur'an, and taught at a *madrasa* in Sivrihisar. The underlying cause for his trips to Akşehir and Konya was most likely a spiritual journey since religious scholars like as Mahmud Hayrani and Seyyid Hacı İbrahim Sultan lived in those areas. Fuat Köprülü also supports this argument in his book titled *Mecmua-i Maarif,* maintaining that Nasreddin Hodja left his village to pledge allegiance to those great Sufis scholars.[72]

Referring to the section on Nasreddin Hodja in *Saltukname,* Ali Günvar argues, "He (Nasreddin Hodja) is one of the dervishes affiliated with Seyyid Mahmud Hayrani. Perhaps he was Hayrani's deputy and served as the dervish of his lodge after Seyyid Mahmud Hayrani passed away."[73]

The century Nasreddin Hodja lived in, the 13th century, is known as both the age of depression and the age of Sufism. The

---

69 Cited by Bekir Şahin, Nasreddin Hoca'nın Felsefesi, *Nasreddin Hoca,* p. 11.

70 İsmail Güleç, "İsmail Emre ve Nasreddin Hoca'nın Fıkralarına Farklı Bir Yaklaşım," *Yedi İklim* dergisi a.g.s. p. 99; See *Yunus Emre and Tasavvuf* by Sabri Erdoğan for further discussion on these arguments. See V. Milletlerarası Türk Halk Kültürü Kongresi Nasreddin Hoca Bildirileri, Ankara 1996.

71 İsmail Güleç, ibid., p. 100

72 M. Fuat Köprülü ibid., p. 22

73 Ali Günvar, ibid., p. 9.

dervishes who immigrated from Turkestan (a mountainous region of Central Asia populated by Turkic people) to Anatolia during the Mongol invasion saw Sufi thought as the unique remedy for the people. The most prominent Sufis of the time were Mawlana Jala-luddin Rumi, Hacı Bektaş-ı Veli, and Yunus Emre. Nasreddin Hodja was the product of the same age. As he lived in Konya for some time, it is likely that he met Rumi.

For these reasons, Nasreddin Hodja was called a saint by many people. The first few people who compiled his jokes referred to him as Nasreddin Hodja, a blessed person.

Based on the historical records and jokes, it is hard to agree with Ali Günvar's description of Nasreddin Hodja as a "sheikh". As another research suggests, a more realistic view would be that, "Nasreddin Hodja was a follower of the Sufi tradition. However, it is hard to derive, based on the available records, that he was a sheikh."[74]

Nasreddin Hodja, as a Sufi (regardless of whether he was a sheikh or an adherent only) was still an idiosyncratic person. First of all, the Sufi worldview saved him from being a bigot or a pedant. Tolerance, empathy and love for others were central to his approach to life. On top of this, he advised people to adopt this philosophy. Although he was a member of a particular dervish order, his under-standing of Sufism never rendered him a hermit or someone oblivi-ous to everyday life. He preferred to live amongst the people.

D. As a Cleric

Nasreddin Hodja served as a prayer leader and preacher in the vil-lage he was born in, Hortu, and in various other places in and around Sivrihisar and Akşehir. He gives rational answers in line with Islamic values and norms and uses articulate language that is easy to comprehend.

---

[74] Alim Yıldız, Nasreddin Hoca'nın Tasavvufi Yönü, *Yedi İklim* ibid., p.103-105.

A woman visited Nasreddin Hodja and asked him to write something to be used an amulet for her defiant daughter. He told the woman, "You see that I am getting older and my breath is not powerful enough to recite a supplication that will curb your daughter's excesses. You'd better find a good husband for her. Her husband can cure her. Besides, if she has a couple of kids, that will keep her quite busy. Your daughter will turn into a woman that is as quiet as an angel."

Nasreddin Hodja also opposed the fatalism that stems from a certain interpretation of religion. While staying in an inn, he recommended that the inn-keeper fix the old ceiling that was about to collapse. The inn-keeper immediately tried to reassure Nasreddin Hodja, "Nasreddin! Don't you know that every thing praises God in its own way? Theo beams in the ceiling are devotedly chanting the names of God; that's why they are stretching." "That's exactly what I am worried about," Nasreddin replied, "They are praying so devoutly that pretty soon they will fall prostrate!"

In a speech he gave in a village Nasreddin Hodja told the people about how Jesus was raised to the heavens. A curious woman asked him what Jesus ate there. Nasreddin Hodja was angry because had been in the village for almost a month had not been offered him any food yet. So he replied, "You silly woman, why do you ask what Jesus eats in heaven when you cannot even remember to ask what poor Nasreddin Hodja eats on the earth!"

Similar examples are manifold, and the core of the issue is that Nasreddin Hodja is a cleric who aims to enlighten people.

E. As a Jurist

Nasreddin Hodja worked as a judge (*qadi*) upon the completion of his *madrasa* education. Thus, he was also a jurist in addition to being a prayer leader, a scholar, and a man of humor; the frequent use of the words "court," "judge," "defendant-plaintiff," and "witness" indicate this.

He was not a type of jurist who issued innovative opinions on jurisprudence. Rather, he applied the existing laws and regulations. He preferred to use plain and unequivocal language to explain his opinions. His intellectual capacity, charming personality, humor, and wit are evident in his judicial opinions.

The following jokes highlight these characteristics of Nasreddin Hodja. Before he returned a verdict, he placed himself in both the defendant's and the plaintiff's shoes. This joke is an example of this:

Two men appeared before Judge Nasreddin Hodja. The first man said, "This man bit my ear. I demand compensation." The second man said, "He bit it himself." Nasreddin Hodja withdrew to his chamber and spent an hour trying to bite his own ear. He succeeded only in falling over and bruising his forehead. Returning to the courtroom, he pronounced, "Examine the man whose ear was bitten. If his forehead is bruised, he did it himself and the case is dismissed. If his forehead is not bruised, the other man did it and must pay compensation."

Nasreddin Hodja was always criticized corrupt jurists. The following shows his attitude toward a corrupt judge:

One day Nasreddin Hodja appealed to the court to make a decision on a case. The presiding judge was known as someone who accepted bribes. Despite his efforts, Nasreddin Hodja was unable to get a decision from the judge since he refused to offer a bribe. Finally, after he gave the judge a pot of honey, the document was issued and the matter was resolved. A few days, the judge looked inside the pot only to find clay under a coating of honey. Angered, he sent a messenger to Nasreddin Hodja who told him, "There was a mistake in the court decision. It needs to be sent back so I can fix the mistake." Nasreddin Hodja responded, "The mistake lies in the personal creed of the judge, not in the court decision. The officers working with him made no mistakes but the honey in the pot can be bad. May God forgive the judge."

Nasreddin Hodja was also annoyed by trivial court cases. Two men appeared before Nasreddin when he was a judge. One man leveled the following accusation at the other: "This man was carrying some wood on his back. However, the poor man tripped on a stone in the road and lost half of his load. I asked the man, 'If I load the fallen pieces of wood back onto your back, what will you give me?' 'Nothing,' the man carrying the wood replied.

This man wanted to be paid for his assistance. Nasreddin Hodja responded to him, "Go lift the corner of the rug and see what is underneath. What do you see?"

"Nothing."

"Take that 'nothing' with you," Nasreddin Hodja said, "That's your compensation!"

F. As an Educator

Nasreddin Hodja was also an educator. His involvement in education was not limited to educating students at the *madrasa*. He also educated the common folk. He evaluated and criticized the deviance and problems in society and pointed out what is right. He did not try to create new theories. Instead, he focused on the implications of the existing education system on individuals and society. When analyzing his educational approach, particular attention should be paid to psychology, the characteristics of the individuals involved, and the societal conditions. Accordingly, he drew attention to the relationship between education and an individual's life. Education was not an abstract domain in his life.

His educational approach, which focused both the education of the individual and of society as a whole, was based on certain principles. Nasreddin believed that an educator should his students' level very well and adjust his teaching methods accordingly.

His educational approach could be considered a model for educators today.

Nasreddin Hodja paid special attention to the individual differences of his students well before his Western colleagues did in the 17th century. Therefore, in line with how the prophets taught their disciples, he modified his teaching style and pace according his audience taking their differences into account. A conversation between Nasreddin Hodja and his stingy neighbor is an example of this:

One day, Nasreddin Hodja's miserly neighbor fell into a lake. The man's friends, trying to save him, shouted, "Give me your hand! Give me your hand!" Despite the risk of drowning, he refused to give his hand to anyone. On seeing this, Nasreddin Hodja shouted, "Take my hand! Take my hand," and saved the man at the last minute. Everybody was surprised and they asked Hodja how he managed to make the man respond to his call. Hodja explained: I know my neighbor's character well. He is such a stingy man that he would not "give" anything to anybody, so I told him to "take" my hand instead.

He did not waste time on discussing trivial scientific details that would not be helpful to his students. He chose to discuss topics based on reason; nothing could draw him into futile discussions. He did not hesitate to teach lessons to those who tried to engage him in vain talk.

The use of punishment in education is still a highly contested issue and not approved of in the modern education system. Nasreddin Hodja shows through the following joke that punishment is not useful as a means to educate people.

When Nasreddin was a student in the *madrasa*, he saw a cane on the wall in a classroom and asked his teacher what it was. The teacher replied, "It is a bastinado which fell from Heaven. It is used to discipline spoiled kids." Not happy with the answer, young Nasreddin continued to ask: "What should be done with something which did not remain in Heaven?" The teacher replied, "it deserves being thrown to Hell." Nasreddin threw the cane into the fireplace.

Seeing that, his teacher thundered, "What happened to the cane?" He replied, "if it did not remain in Heaven, then it deserves being thrown to Hell" That's why I threw it into the fire!"

Laziness is another issue that Nasreddin tried to combat. The following joke illustrates his attitude toward work-shy people:

One day, Nasreddin Hodja was on the roof of his house, fixing a hole in the tiles. Suddenly, he heard someone call, "Hello!" When he looked down, Hodja saw an old man in dirty clothing standing below. "What do you want?" Nasreddin asked. "Come down and I'll tell you," said the man. Nasreddin was annoyed, but he was a polite man so he put down his tools. He carefully climbed all the way down to the ground. "What do you want?" he asked when he reached the ground. "Could you spare a little money for this poor guy?" asked the old man. Nasreddin thought for a minute and then said, "Come with me." He started to climb the ladder again. The old man followed him all the way to the top. When they were both sitting on the roof, Nasreddin turned to the beggar. "No," he said. The beggar was annoyed and exclaimed, "You are such a cruel man. Did you have me climb up the ladder only to say this?" "It is you who is cruel!" Nasreddin replied, "It was OK for you to call me down to ask for money and not fair when I call you up!"[75]

---

[75] See *Bir Eğitimci Olarak Nasreddin Hoca* by Abdullah Özbek, Konya 2004 for a comprehensive description of Nasreddin Hodja as an educator.

CHAPTER FIVE

Nasreddin Hodja in the
East and the West

"...Nasreddin Hodja has been internationally recognized since the 15th century in countries in Central Asia, including but not limited to Azerbaijan and Turkmenistan. His fame also travelled to the land of Uighurs, China, India, and during Ottoman rule, to the Balkans and Europe. Arabs attributed many jokes of Nasreddin Hodja to Juha and translated them to Arabic. Meanwhile, Nasreddin Hodja became the shared cultural icon of the world's people and is known by various names."

Dr. Mehmet Önder

NASREDDIN HODJA IN THE
EAST AND THE WEST

The Lands Where Nasreddin Hodja Is Recognized

N asreddin Hodja is famous in many different places. During the rule of the Ottoman Empire, his reputation and jokes spread from Anatolia to the rest of the Middle East, the Caucasus, Central Asia, the Balkans, and North Africa.[76]

This fame caused people from different countries to claim ownership on this legendary character. Similarly, joke tellers that can be called "twins of Nasreddin Hodja" popped up in different places.

There are a number of reasons that account for this spread of Nasreddin Hodja's fame. The primary reason is the oral tradition. Merchants, statesmen, and travelers carried his jokes from their homeland to numerous other places. In addition, because of the settlement policy of the Ottomans, a considerable number of Turkish Muslims moved to the Balkans and brought Nasreddin Hodja's jokes with them.[77] This was made easier by the fact that the people who moved to the Balkans knew Turkish and this facilitated the transmission of his jokes.

A. The Turkic World

Nasreddin Hodja is widely known in the Turkic world. As Fuat Köprülü puts it, "Nasreddin Hodja has been recognized for centu-

---

[76] Mustafa Duman, *Yedi İklim* dergisi, Bulgaristan'da Nasreddin Hoca ve Kurnaz Peter p. 53.

[77] Hayriye Süleymanoğlu Yenisey, Rumeli'de Nasreddin Hoca, *Yedi İklim*. p. 64.

ries by the Islamic tribes of the East, especially among the Turks who were spread all around Europe and Asia. Not only the great thinkers, but the lay people, villagers, and even immigrants knew him very well."[78]

In the Turkic world, Nasreddin Hodja was either called by his actual name or his name was rendered into the local language. For instance, the Azeris called him "Molla" or "Mulla Nasreddin;" the Turkmen "Hoca Ependi," "Efendi," or "Nasreddin Ependi;" and the Uzbeks called him "Hoca Nasriddin," "Nasriddin," "Afandi," or "Efendi." He was known as "Hoca Nasir," "Mulla Nasriddin," or "Hoca Mulla Nasreddin" among the Kazakhs while the Uighurs called him "Nasreddin Efendi" or "Efendi-Ependi." The Gagauz Turks called him "Bizim Nastradin" or "Nasradın Hoca" and Turks living in the Balkans referred to him as "Nastratin Hoca."

The Uighur Turks who called him "Hoca Nasreddin" were influential in spreading his name to China and Taiwan. The Taiwanese called him "Hoca," "Molla Nasreddin," "Oca," or "Anastratin."

It is not unexpected to find the so-called twins of Nasreddin Hodja, famous for their jokes, in the regions mentioned so far. For example, the Turkmen have Kâmine, the Karakalpak have Ömür-beg Lakki, the Tajiks have Müşfikî, and the Crimeans have Ahmet Akay. The similarities between these people and Nasreddin Hodja are astonishing.[79]

B. OTHER MUSLIM COUNTRIES

Nasreddin Hodja has also been recognized by the non-Turkish Muslim population in the Middle East, Asia and Africa.

He is called "Juha" in northern Africa region and the Arab peninsula. Juha is known as a humorous figure in Islamic culture

---

[78] M. Fuat Köprülü, *Nasreddin Hoca*, p. 184-185.

[79] Türker Acaroğlu, Nasreddin Hoca'nın İkiz Kardeşleri, 1. Milletlerarası Nasreddin Hoca Sempozyum Bildirileri [Proceedings of the International Symposia on Nasreddin Hodja].

throughout the Arab-Muslim world. According to some accounts, Juha is Nasreddin Hodja. Historical records do not show any proof of a real person named Juha.[80] Still, others maintain that Juha and Nasreddin Hodja could either be the same person or two different historical figures. Regardless of the truth, the fact is that Nasreddin Hodja is well-known in these regions as well.[81]

Nasreddin Hodja is also known in India, Bangladesh, Nepal, Sri Lanka, and Burma. The Pakistani people were responsible for spreading the jokes of Nasreddin Hodja to these areas. Nasreddin holds a special place in Pakistani culture where he is known as "Mulla Nasuriddin". There are a number of individuals, including "Şeyh Çilli" and "Molla Dupiyaza" who told jokes similar to those of Nasreddin Hodja.[82] He is also called "Lal Bucakkar" and "Birbal" in Sri Lanka and Nepal.[83] In Iran, Nasreddin is called "Juha" and "Molla Nasreddin" while he is known as "Jeha" in the Berber countries of northern Africa. He is called "Jahan" in Malta, "Jinf" in Sicily, and "Hioha" or "Jovani" in Calabria.

C. In the West

Nasreddin Hodja is also popular in many European countries, particularly in the Balkans. Therefore, the Bulgarians, Greeks, Serbians, Croatians, Montenegrins, Bosnians, Albanians, Kosovars, and Romanians are all familiar with Nasreddin Hodja's jokes. Nasreddin Hodja has become an integral part of folk literatures in this area and numerous books on him have been published in this region.[84]

---

80 Abdul Kayyum Can, Dış Yurtlarda Nasreddin Hoca, III. Uluslararası Halk edebiyatı Semineri Bildirileri [Proceedings of the 3rd Annual International Folk Literature Symposium] p. 81.

81 Yakup Civelek, Cuha; Arapların Nasreddin Hocası, *Yedi İklim* p. 120.

82 Masud Akhtar Shaikh, Nasreddin Hoca Pakistan'da, *Yedi İklim*, ibid., p. 154.

83 Gönül Yonar Utku, Doğu ve Batı Ülkelerinde Nasreddin Hoca, *Yedi İklim*, ibid., p. 167.

84 M. Türker Acaroğlu, Nasreddin Hoca Balkanlarda, III. Uluslararası Halk Edebiyatı Semineri Bildirileri [Proceedings of the 3rd Annual International Folk Literature Symposium] p. 15-39.

His fame also reached France, Germany, Italy, the Czech Republic, Slovakia, and the United States.

Nasreddin Hodja is either called by his own name or by the name of one his so-called twins. For instance, the Germans call him "Till Eulenspiegel," a popular hero. The Bulgarians call him "Hiter (clever) Peter," the Hungarians "Ludas Mati," the Serbians "Ero," the Macedonians "Iter Peyo," the Finns "Anti Puuhaara,", and the Italians "Bertoldo."

Nasreddin Hodja has been the subject of novels, movies, plays, and stories in many of these countries as well as in caricatures and paintings. In addition, it is also possible to find articles on him in the media.

CHAPTER SIX

The Jokes of Nasreddin Hoca

"The jokes of Nasreddin Hodja occupy a special place in our culture of jokes. His name is so closely connected to jokes and humor that he is the first person that comes to mind when thinking of jokes. No joke can be considered a perfect joke if it does not reference Nasreddin Hodja."

Dr. Saim Sakaoğlu

THE JOKES OF NASREDDIN HOCA

A. COMPILATIONS

T he essential reason for Nasreddin Hodja's worldwide fame is his jokes. The actual number of his jokes is unknown as he did not write a book himself.

His jokes, which were orally transmitted to the subsequent generations, were later written down. Therefore, the total number of Nasreddin Hodja jokes differs depending on time and place. The number is inflated as people commonly attribute the jokes of others to Hodja, as is the case with other popular figures like the Anatolian Sufi Yunus Emre.

Starting in the early fifteenth century, the jokes of Nasreddin Hodja began to be compiled in written form. It is not known who the first person was to compile his jokes and when they were gathered in book form for the first time.

According to the current scholars the first written source was *Saltukname* (1480), which describes the fame of Nasreddin Hodja and explains that his jokes were compiled in books.

Hâzâ Hikâyat-ı Kitâb-ı Nasreddin is the oldest written collection of Nasreddin Hodja's jokes, not including the jokes in *Saltukname*. This book, written by a person called Hüseyin in 1571, includes 43 of Nasreddin's jokes. *Letâif'i Nasreddin Hoca*, written by Mehmed in 1676, contains 112 jokes. Mehmed Gazali, Güvahi, Lamii Çelebi and Taşlıcalı Yahya Bey are also among the early compilers of Nasreddin Hodja's jokes. Today, there are more than fifty different compilations of Nasreddin Hodja's jokes.

Since the 16th century, many different efforts have been taken to compile jokes. The earliest compilation, written in 1571, is *Hâzâ Hikâyat-ı Kitab-ı Nasreddin*.

Scholars are still compiling Nasreddin Hodja's jokes today, and thus, the total number of jokes attributed to him has increased. For instance, a book printed in 1968 included 445 of his jokes.

The first literary collection of Nasreddin Hodja's jokes was compiled by Mehmet Tevfik Bey.[85] Also known by his pseodonym, *Çaylak* (Novice), he retold approximately 200 of Nasreddin Hodja's jokes in literary form in his books: *Letâif-i Nasreddin, Bû Âdem* (1881–1883), and *Hazine-i Letâif* (1884–1885). *Letâif-i Nasreddin,* illustrated with pictures, was the first book that included both Nasreddin's biography as well as his jokes. Similar collections were published in the following years. Several lithographs, some of which were illustrated, were printed before and after the Republican era. In 1926, Veled Çelebi İzbudak[86] compiled Nasreddin Hodja's jokes, and the book was published under the title *Letaif-i Nasreddin Hoca.*

Nasreddin Hodja's jokes have been translated into several major languages. However, people in different regions were familiar with his jokes even before they were translated due to oral tradition; the Anatolian people who travelled and immigrated to other places, bringing Nasreddin Hodja's jokes with them. Nasreddin Hodja was either referred to using his real name or with a local name such as Juha in the Arab countries and Peter around the Balkans. However, it was not until UNESCO declared 1996 "the year of Nasreddin Hodja" that Nasreddin Hodja became known around

---

85 Çaylak Tevfik's (1843–1892) real name was Mehmet Tevfik. His nickname comes from *Çaylak* [The Novice], the humor magazine he published titled . He compiled jokes of Nasreddin Hodja.

86 Veled Çelebi İzbudak (Çelebi Mehmed Bahaüddin)(1869–1953) was a poet, linguist and a man of letters. His father was one of Rumi's grandsons. He translated several works, including *Mathnawi* by Rumi. He also translated a book of Nasreddin Hodja's jokes.

the world. The amount of research on him has greatly increased since then.[87]

B. THE BASIC CHARACTERISTICS

It is essential to examine Nasreddin Hodja's jokes in terms of both form and content. The jokes consist a brief story or event and some information about the characters and the setting is provided. The joke concludes with a witty message.

Regarding the content, the main subject is always a human being. Man's ridiculous and selfish character as well as mistakes, vices, awkwardness, and despair are addressed in a humorous but tangible way. Poverty is another recurring theme and issues related to human relationship are also touched upon.

Nasreddin Hodja addressed these issues while showing deep love and respect for people, society, the environment, and other living creatures. He was never contemptuous or mocking. He criticized the bad behavior and thoughts of people with the purpose of helping people realize their mistakes before they hurt the feelings of others.

Nasreddin Hodja offered clever solutions to a wide variety of social issues in his jokes. In addition to social vices such as ignorance, selfishness, thievery, self-interestedness, and excessive love for this world; issues such as oppressive and unjust rulers, corrupt officials, the detachment of scholars from the people, the bigotry of some clergymen, the characteristics of a good cleric, the relationship with God, the pillars of faith and practice of religion were among the common topics addressed in his jokes.

The nature of the issues addressed in his jokes indicates that the main purpose of Nasreddin's humorous stories was not entertainment. He knew how to use humor to make people think. In his struggle against bad behavior, he tried to draw attention to such be-

---

[87] See Alpay Kabacalı for a list of research on Nasreddin Hodja. *Bütün Yönleriyle Nasreddin Hoca*, p. 108–112.

havior through the use of humor. It is important to note that he did not intend to mock or humiliate anyone or any group of people in his stories.

Another important feature of his jokes is that the emphasis on moral values. He was not verbose; he tended to abstain from using fancy words and abundant descriptive narratives. He spoke in the everyday language of the people. However, due to the nature of the topics addressed, he did on occasion use some Arabic and Persian words.

Nasreddin Hodja's jokes reflect the social reality of Anatolian society of the time. The main themes of the jokes, the characters, and heroes as well as the messages conveyed are directly related to the social conditions and happenings of the era.

C. Determining the Authenticity

Some scholars have developed a list of specific criteria that will enable researchers to better understand Nasreddin Hodja's jokes and to be able to distinguish the authentic jokes from those attributed to him. Şükrü Kurgan created the following indicators to help a researcher determine if the joke is authentic:

a) If a joke is about intoxication or alcohol, the joke does not belong to Nasreddin Hodja as his jokes are compatible with Islamic values and ethics.

b) If a character saves himself/herself by acting foolish or hiding his/her wit, it is not one of his jokes.

c) If Nasreddin Hodja is described as an affluent person and a slave owner who dines on golden plates, the joke is not Nasreddin Hodja's as he lived in poverty for his entire life.

d) If a joke contains themes such as lust, promiscuity and betrayal, it is not one of Nasreddin's.

e) If a joke depicts Nasreddin as a parsimonious person, it is not one of his jokes since he constantly criticizes misery.

f) If Nasreddin Hodja is depicted as a powerful and wealthy person who overcomes problems through the use of might, this joke does not belong to Nasreddin as he tended to solve problems using his intelligence.

g) If such vices as flattery, hypocrisy and self-interestedness are found in the joke, or if Nasreddin is described as a person who works for a pasha or a powerful person, this joke is not authentic.

h) If Nasreddin Hodja is portrayed as an intractable and obstinate person who forces people to act as he wishes, the joke is not an original.

i) If a joke is about Sufism, timelessness and eternity, that joke does not belong to Hodja as he considered these topics to be too serious to be used in jokes.

j) Lastly, if a joke is verbose and excessively long (if it takes several minutes to tell the joke), this joke is not authentic.[88]

According to another expert, the following are the common characteristics found fin Nasreddin Hodja's jokes:

Subtlety, politeness, discretion and reasonableness, decency, modesty, frankness, tolerance, empathy, optimism, peaceful coexistence, self-esteem, and the satire of coarseness, selfishness, ill-intentions, vanity, and affectation. There is also criticism of superstitious beliefs, laziness, social parasites, and unnecessary red tape. In addition, we see an effort to train the carnal self, and careful attention not to judge people based on their outlook.[89]

D. How to Interpret the Jokes

It is crucial to be familiar with Nasreddin Hodja's personality, his level of knowledge, and his relation to his faith as well as the general characteristics of the places, people, lifestyle and standards of

---

[88] Şükrü Kurgan, *Nasreddin Hoca Fıkralarında Türk Halk Yaşayışının İzleri* p. 494–496.
[89] Mehmet Aydın, *Nasreddin Hoca* p. 56.

the time, and the symbolism embedded in the culture in order to fully understand his jokes. The essence of the jokes cannot be fully captured if these details are ignored. Failure to pay attention to these details may result in the misreading and misunderstanding of Nasreddin Hodja's joke.

The following joke is attributed to Nasreddin Hodja: One day Hodja came across a group of people in Akşehir staring at a point in the distance. He approached the group and asked them what they were looking at. "We are watching the crescent (to see whether it is time to fast since fasting starts based on the position of the moon)," replied someone from the group. "The people of Akşehir are such weird people. You gathered here just to see a tiny crescent. People in Sivrihisar do not bother to look at the moon even if they see the moon is as big as the wheel of a car," Nasreddin Hodja said.

At first sight, one may tend to deduce that people of Sivrihisar would be oblivious to fasting which is one of the basic pillars of Islam. However, this could not be the case since there were also Christians living in Sivrihisar at that time. Therefore, Hodja wants to point out that the Christian people in Sivrihisar do not practice fasting during the month of Ramadan. If the reader is unaware that Christians also lived in Sivrihisar piece of information is missing, one might arrive at a misleading conclusion.

E. DIFFERENT VIEWS ON NASREDDIN HODJA AND HIS JOKES

"Nature and society are the two basic sources of Nasreddin Hodja's jokes. The majority of his jokes carry universal realities that set examples for all time periods and people. Every societal issue is covered in his jokes since people sought his guidance in religious, economic, educational, and judicial topics as well as in human relations." *(Ahmet Kabaklı)*[90]

---

[90] *Türk Edebiyatı* dergisi, ibid., p. 7.

"There is a strong sense individualism in Nasreddin Hodja's jokes that stems from his character. We feel this character come alive when we hear his jokes. A certain world view can be discerned in his jokes. He is a joyful, fatherly yet controversial person who acts in line with conventional wisdom. Nevertheless, his humor is not as destructive as satire. He is the symbol of good intentions." (*Ahmet Kutsi Tecer*)[91]

"Nasreddin Hodja is the mirror of society. His jokes are the human silhouettes reflected in that mirror. We, as human beings, are see all our differences and paradoxes in these reflections as well as our beliefs, apathy, submission and insurgence, hopes and pessimism, courage and cowardice, love and hatred, intelligence and foolishness, our thoughts and smiling faces, and our tolerance and cruelty. In short, we are reflected on that mirror with all our characteristics including our most private thoughts." (*N. Ahmet Özalp*)[92]

"At least seven Nasreddin Hodja jokes should be told at any gathering since every joke reveals wisdom and beauty. Rather than telling only a single joke, telling a few jokes may be stimulating, thought-provoking and could lead to analytical thinking. This will simultaneously lead to more fun and more contemplation and will turn out to be the natural flow of life." (*A. Haydar Haksal*)[93]

"Nasreddin Hodja, who paints a picture of a sagacious and humorous Turkish layman who embraces an optimistic worldview through concise tales and answers, is a popular yet unconventional philosopher. He comes up with practical solutions to people's daily problems on with a tolerant perspective free from harsh judgments." (*Behçet Necatigil*)[94]

"The good thing about Nasreddin Hodja's jokes is that they are composed of the sort of incidents that were likely to happen in the society he lived in. Due to this, we are enable to discern that

---

[91] *İslâm Ansiklopedisi*, vol. 9 p.109.

[92] *Yedi İklim* dergisi, ibid., p. 2.

[93] *Yedi İklim* dergisi, ibid., p. 22.

[94] Behçet Necatigil, *Edebiyatımızda İsimler Sözlüğü*, p. 199.

the jokes not compatible with the realities of his time cannot be attributed to him." (*Selçuk Çıkla*)[95]

"No satire or mockery is found in Nasreddin Hodja's jokes. They are simple and modest, and the affairs of the people, as well as their joy, despair, peculiarities, disagreements, and conflicts constitute the subject matter of Nasreddin Hodja's stories." (*Nejat Muallimoğlu*)[96]

"Neither did Nasreddin Hodja focus on the absurdities of life nor did he use meaningless and rude examples of humor like others did. It was not his words, but his soul and worldview that created his jokes. He detected the essence of the incidents with his soul and was able to make them funny. He laughed at these things and made everyone laugh at them." (*Eflatun Cem Güney*)[97]

"Historians, literary critics, sociologists and even theologians should study Nasreddin Hodja. His jokes are not mere tools for fun; they are the documents fraught with wisdom, virtue, propriety and exemplars. It leads one to contemplate and learn." (*M. Halistin Kukul*)[98]

---

[95] *Yedi İklim* dergisi, ibid., p. 2, 4, 22, 144.
[96] *Türk Edebiyatı* dergisi, ibid., p. 27.
[97] Eflatun Cem Güney, ibid., p. 214.
[98] *Türk Edebiyatı* dergisi, ibid., p. 69.

CHAPTER SEVEN

Some Examples of
Nasreddin Hodja's Jokes

"Nasreddin Hodja is a symbol of the Turkish people. His jokes are short. He tackles individuals and society's serious issues. His jokes make one ponder, laugh, and learn. You get the sense of irony but you never feel offended."

Kemal Uzun

SOME EXAMPLES OF
NASREDDIN HODJA'S JOKES

A. IN PROSE

1. Jokes about his Donkey

Nasreddin Hodja's donkey held a special place in his jokes; therefore, there are countless jokes about his donkey. Like any other person who lived in that era, his donkey played an integral role in his life. Most people used their donkeys for transportation; only affluent people rode horses. Thus, owning a donkey categorized a person as being average.

Nasreddin did not get along well with his donkey; they always had a rocky relationship. Nasreddin Hodja was often put in strange situations due to the stubbornness of his donkey. In addition, his donkey was also affected poverty and was hungry most of the time. For this reason, it was a source of concern for him.

Nasreddin's problematic relationship with his donkey indicates that in the jokes the donkey signifies ignorance and rudeness. The donkey reminds people of vices, such as stubbornness.

The donkey still has a similar symbolism in today's culture. As one scholar put it, "There was no better symbol that would describe the state of an average person struggling with chaos and immersed in ignorance, ambivalence, and superstitions better than donkey." [99] In addition, the Qur'an (Jumua 62:5) refers to those who do not

---

[99] Şaban Abak, ibid., p. 15.

practice what the divine scriptures teach them as donkeys carrying books. The following joke provides a good example of this:

One day, while Nasreddin Hodja was talking to a group of people, he claimed that he taught his donkey how to read. Some people from the group did not believe him and stated that it is impossible to teach a donkey to read. So Nasreddin put a thick book in front of the donkey. He had placed some grain inside the book beforehand and had taught the donkey to turn the pages with its nose to find it. The donkey started to turn the pages one by one trying to find the grain before it reached the last page. "Did you see? It just finished reading," said Nasreddin Hodja. The people in the crowd complained, "Yes, it read the book, but nobody understood what it read." Nasreddin replied, "It read the book in donkey language, and one needs to know that language to be able to understand what it read."

Samples of Nasreddin Hodja's Jokes

Hodja's Destination

One day Nasreddin Hodja was riding his donkey. No matter how hard he tried, he was not able to turn the head of the stubborn donkey toward where he wanted to go.

Seeing this, his neighbor asked: "

Where are you heading Hodja?"

"Wherever my donkey wants to go," replied Nasreddin Hodja.

The Joy of Finding Something

One day Nasreddin Hodja lost his donkey. He rushed to the marketplace and announced that his donkey was lost, "I will give my donkey and his saddle to whoever finds him and brings him to me."

Some people questioned Nasreddin Hodja, "Why are you looking for him in the first place if you want to give him away after he is found?"

"Oh!" he replied, "You don't know the joy of finding something you have lost!"

The Grey Donkey

Nasreddin Hodja had a grey donkey which was very irritable. For this reason, Nasreddin decided to sell the donkey.

He took the obstinate donkey to the market to sell it. When a person approached to check its teeth, the donkey bit his hand. Another man tried to mount the donkey and was kicked. The donkey continued to behave this way. After observing the situation, the head salesman in the market told Nasreddin Hodja, "This wild donkey either bites or kicks potential customers. It seems like nobody will want to buy it. Who would want to own such a troublesome donkey?"

"My dear friend! I did not bring this donkey here to sell it," said Nasreddin.

"Why did you bring it then?" asked the man curiously.

Nasreddin Hodja took a look at the donkey and nodded his head desperately, "I wanted people to see what I was going through."

Backwards on the Donkey

One day Nasreddin Hodja was riding his donkey facing backwards. Curious people asked, "Why do you ride your donkey facing backwards?"

"I did not want to see that I was heading in the same direction as the donkey."

The Missing Donkey

One day Nasreddin Hodja couldn't find his donkey and set off to look for it. While he was searching for it, he was also giving thanks to God out loud. People asked him what he was so grateful for. "What if I had been on the donkey when he got lost!" replied Nasreddin Hodja.

The Donkey and the Horse

One day Nasreddin Hodja was going somewhere on his donkey. A wealthy acquaintance, who was riding an ostentatious horse, caught up with him. He was looking for an opportunity to show off his horse and belittle Nasreddin Hodja.

"Nasreddin Hodja, how is the donkey moving?" asked the man in a mocking tone.

Hodja shouted back: "The donkey is riding a horse!"

2. Jokes about Thieves and Beggars

Thievery is a vice in which is part of every society. Yet, thievery becomes much more prevalent in societies where people live in abject poverty. In addition to being immoral, it is also the result of a weak economy. The society Nasreddin Hodja lived in was going through financial difficulties and poverty was the number one issue at the time. People had experienced famine for many years. As a result, both Nasreddin Hodja and his neighbors were victims of theft.

Samples of Nasreddin Hodja's Jokes

Let Him Take Whatever He Can Find

One night a burglar broke into Hodja's house.

His wife whispered, "Nasreddin, do you hear footsteps? I think there is a thief inside. Let's check it out!

Nasreddin Hodja responded, "

Don't even bother! I wish he could find something to steal. It would be easy to take it back from him."

Who is at fault?

One day Nasreddin Hodja's house was robbed. His neighbors accused him of not fixing the door and not building the wall high enough in the backyard. Others found other reasons to explain why his house was robbed.

Fed up with the accusations, Nasreddin Hodja shouted, "

Yes, you are right! Those are my faults. But am I the only one to blame? Is the thief totally innocent?"

Trick

One day Nasreddin Hodja plotted against his miserly neighbor. He took the man's goose while it was asleep and hid it under his robe.

After a long period of silence, Hodja thought that the goose might have died due to lack of oxygen. He opened his robe and checked to see if the goose was still alive. As soon as he opened his robe, the goose hissed.

"Good boy! You are smarter than the man who owns you. I was going to tell you to keep quiet and you told me to hush."

Mercy!

One day a thief broke into Nasreddin Hodja's house and slipped off his shoes to avoid making noise. However Nasreddin Hodja returned home and hid the thief's shoes. When he didn't find anything to steal, the thief left. As he couldn't find his shoes he had to leave the house barefoot.

Nasreddin Hodja shouted, "Catch that shameless thief, he is running away!"

When Nasreddin's neighbors caught the thief, the thief complained, "Have mercy on me! I broke into his house, yet Nasreddin Hodja stole my shoes."

Nothing Left to Steal

Thieves frequently broke into Nasreddin Hodja's house. They stole everything Hodja had.

One day a thief again broke into his house. He entered a room only to find it empty, and when he looked in another room he found nothing. Finally, in the last room, he found Nasreddin Hodja sitting with his hands covering his face.

Not knowing what to do next, the thief asked,

"Hodja! What are you doing in this dark room on your own?"

"What can I do, my son? I am so embarrassed that you are going to leave this house empty-handed. That's why I am hiding here!" he said.

3. Jokes about Nasreddin Hodja's wives

Nasreddin Hodja was married twice. In fact, as one of his jokes reveals, he lived together with his wives for a period of time. Nasreddin did not get along well with his wives; they always had problems. However, his problematic relationship with his wives contradicts his cheerful, well-mannered, reasonable, and pleasant personality.

This category of jokes is important as it provides information about the status of women in the patriarchal society. It is possible that the turbulent nature of the era as well as the financial difficulties Nasreddin face played a role in his problematic relationship with his wives. However, he does not complain about them even though he seems discontent with the situation. He is as tender and understanding toward his wives as he is toward other people. He corrects his wives' mistakes which stem from lack of knowledge without belittling her.

Samples of the Jokes about his wives

Afraid of his wife

One day Nasreddin Hodja was discussing with friends whether one should be afraid of his wife or not. Someone from the group proposed, "Those who are afraid of their wives should stay seated and those who are not should stand up."

Nasreddin Hodja did not stand up, and others asked him, " Nasreddin Hodja, are you afraid of your wife?"

"Of course, I am. Didn't you see that my legs trembled so much that I could not even get up?"

The Cost of Feeding the Donkey

Nasreddin Hodja and his wife were both sick and tired of feeding their donkey. They argued over who was to feed the donkey and made a bet. Whoever spoke first had to feed the donkey. Nasreddin Hodja was determined not to lose. One day, while his wife was visiting a neighbor, a burglar broke into their house. Nasreddin was home, but kept silent so as to not lose the bet. The thief packed everything up and left the house. When Nasreddin's wife returned to home to an empty house, she shouted, "Oh my God! What happened?" Nasreddin Hodja grinned with delight, "I won the bet! Now you have to feed the donkey."

Return from the Wedding

One day Nasreddin Hodja returned from work very tired. His wife greeted him with a sullener face than usual.

Seeing she was in a very bad mood, he asked, "What's up? Is something wrong?"

"You know that our neighbor was sick," said the wife.

"What happened to her," he asked.

"She passed away."

"Oh, I am so sorry to hear that," said Nasreddin Hodja. He added, "You have the same sullen face you have even when you return from a wedding ceremony."

The Robe

Nasreddin Hodja's neighbors asked him, "We heard noises from your home last night. What happened?"

"My wife was angry and she threw my robe down the stairs," he said.

The neighbors were puzzled, "How can a robe make such a loud noise? They asked.

Nasreddin Hodja replied: "I was wearing the robe when she threw it!"

She Never Had It

One of Nasreddin Hodja's friends told him, "Nasreddin, they say your wife has lost her mind."

– He didn't respond and thought deeply.

The man asked,

"What are you thinking about, Nasreddin?"

"I know that my wife was never a sane person. I am wondering what else she might have lost," he answered.

The Blue Bead

Nasreddin Hodja had two wives. They frequently asked him which one of them he liked the most, and put him in an awkward position. One day he secretly gave each wife a blue bead and instructed them not to tell the other about the gift.

One day the wives asked him, "Which of us do you like the most?"

After giving them both a meaningful look, he answered, "I love the one who has the blue bead the most," and both were satisfied.

Why Don't You Ask Me About Her?

One day Nasreddin Hodja's wife passed away. After the funeral prayer, the imam (prayer leader) questioned the attendees (as is Islamic tradition): "How do you know the deceased, was she a good person?"

"God bless her! She was a good person," they answered.

Upon hearing this response, Nasreddin Hodja stepped forward and complained, "How do they know my wife? Why are you asking them? Ask me about her, and I'll tell you what kind person she was!"

4. Jokes about Nasreddin Hodja's Children

Nasreddin Hodja was the father of a son and a daughter. He mentions them in a couple jokes although most of his jokes are about society at large. His family affairs were private which might account for why the number of jokes pertaining to society is greater than that the number of jokes about his immediate family.

Jokes about Nasreddin Hodja's Children

The Pitcher

One day Nasreddin Hodja sent his son to the fountain to fill up their earthenware water pitcher. After handing him the pitcher, he slapped him, and added, "Do not break the pitcher!"

The people who witnessed this showed their disapproval, "Nasreddin Hodja, the child did not break the pitcher. He has not even left for the fountain yet. Why did you slap him?"

"Because it will be too late if I slap him after he breaks the pitcher!" said Nasreddin.

The Baby Starling

One day, some people asked Nasreddin Hodja's son a question, "What is an eggplant?"His son replied, "It is a baby starling whose eyes have not opened yet."

Upon hearing his son's response, Nasreddin said, "That's his own answer. I did not teach him that."

What Day of Ramadan Is It Today?

During the month of Ramadan (the Muslim month of fasting), Nasreddin Hodja had the habit of putting a pebble in an earthenware pot each morning to count the days of fasting. However, his mischievous daughter saw his father's pot and put two handfuls of pebbles in it.

One day, some people asked him, "Nasreddin Hodja, do you know what day of Ramadan it is today?"

"Just a minute! I have been counting them. I'll check and tell you exactly," he said.

He took out all the pebbles and counted them. There were 120 pebbles. Hodja knew this couldn't be right.

When he got back to his friends, he told that it was the 45th of Ramadan.

The people were baffled, "Nasreddin Hodja, it could not possibly be the 45th of Ramadan. You know that there are only 30 days in a month."

"My dear friends, you better believe me! Because if you rely on the pot, then today it is the 129th of Ramadan!" replied Nasreddin Hodja.

Nasreddin Hodja's Will

Towards the end of his life, Nasreddin Hodja kept telling his children, "Bury me on top of an old grave."

When the children asked him why he wanted to be buried on top of an old grave, he reasoned, "When the angels call me to account, I will tell them that I have already been questioned."

His Stubborn Son

Nasreddin Hodja's son was as stubborn as a mule. He tended to do just the opposite of what he was told. When his wife kept complaining about their son, Nasreddin tried to soothe her, "Take it easy, my dear wife! At least he is predictable. We know very well how he is going to respond to everything we say. Things might be better if we tell him just the opposite of what we really want him to do."

This method proved to be very effective. One day Nasreddin Hodja and his son were on their way to home from the mill house. As they crossed the river Nasreddin recognized that the flour sack was leaning toward left and was about to fall off the donkey's back.

Knowing his son very well, he said, "My dear son! The sack is sliding to the right. You'd better move it to the left."

But contrary to Nasreddin Hodja's expectations, his son did what exactly his father told asked and the sack fell in the river.

Nasreddin got angry at his son, "What did you do? The flour sack is soaked."

"I just wanted to do to what you asked me once a while but it did not work," said his son.

Mom will cry!

Nasreddin Hodja's older son was a potter in a nearby village. One day When Nasreddin visited him, his son told him, "Dad, I spent my fortune on these pots. If it is sunny and they dry in time, I'll be rich. But if it rains, my mom will cry." (This is a Turkish idiom which means to experience great difficulty.)

Nasreddin then paid a visit to his younger son who lived in another village. His son told him, "Dad, I spent all my money on this farm. If it rains in time, I'll become rich. But if there happens to be a drought, my mom will cry."

Nasreddin returned home glum. His wife inquired, "What happened, Nasreddin? Why are you so sullen today?"

"Don't worry about me. You should worry about yourself. It doesn't matter whether it rains or not. You, the mother of our sons, will cry either way.

Hot Soup and Teardrops

After Nasreddin Hodja's wife passed away, it was his duty to cook for their children. One day he made soup and he invited his son to have some with him.

His son was so impatient that didn't realize that the soup was still boiling hot. It was he who took the first spoonful. When he burned his mouth, tears rolled down his face. Nasreddin Hodja asked him why he was crying. "I just remembered my mother, may she rest in peace. She used to love this soup a lot," responded the son.

As he spoke, Nasreddin Hodja took a spoonful of the soup. He burnt his mouth and tears ran down his face.

"Why are you crying?" asked his son, teasing his father.

Trying to conceal his anger, he responded, "Well, I am crying because your mom was such a kind-hearted person. She died and left such a son behind."

5. Jokes about the Children and Youth in the Neighborhood

Nasreddin Hodja also had a good relationship with the children and youth in his neighborhood. He was so understanding and affectionate toward them that they sometimes took advantage of him. But of course, he was still able to teach them something.

Samples of Nasreddin Hodja's Jokes

Turban

One day Nasreddin Hodja was watching the children play in his neighborhood while thinking about his own childhood. When he joined in their game, one of the mischievous children grabbed his turban and threw it to his friends. No matter how hard he tried, Nasreddin was not able to get his turban back. Out of breath, Nasreddin begged the children to return his turban. However, the mischievous children did not seem to care and kept playing with it.

Finally, he gave up and left on his donkey. The people he encountered on his way home asked him, "What is going on, Nasreddin Hodja? Where is your turban?"

"My turban remembered its childhood and is now playing with the children in the street," he replied smiling.

Nasreddin Hodja's Shoes

One day the neighborhood children decided to steal Nasreddin Hodja's shoes.

They invited him under a tree and teased him, "You can't climb this huge tree."

"I can," said Nasreddin Hodja putting his shoes on his belly.

"What are you going to do with your shoes when you are on the tree," the children asked.

"There may be a road to an unknown place up there. That's why I'd better keep them with me, replied Nasreddin Hodja.

Grapes

One day Hodja was returning from the vineyard with a basketful of grapes when the neighborhood children saw him. They gathered around him, asked for grapes. As there were a lot of children, he picked up a bunch of grapes, broke it into pieces, and gave each child one of the pieces. If he gave each child a whole bunch, he would not have any grapes left in the basket.

The children complained, "You have a lot, but you give us only a little!"

"It does not make any difference whether you have a basketful or a small amount. They all taste the same," he responded.

Intermingled Feet in Water

The neighborhood children were sitting by the pool with their feet in the water. When Nasreddin Hodja passed by, the mischievous kids cried for help.

"Nasreddin Hodja, Nasreddin Hodja! Please help us," they screamed all at once.

"Our feet are all mixed up, we don't know which is which. We cannot get out of the water if you do not help us figure out which foot belongs to whom."

Nasreddin Hodja was not about to be outwitted by children. He grabbed a stick and poked the children's legs. Startled by the touch of the stick, the children jumped out of the water with a shriek.

"See? Now you all have found your respective feet," said Nasreddin Hodja.

Doomsday Tomorrow

It had been a long time since the youngsters in Nasreddin Hodja's neighborhood had a good feast. They plotted to make him treat them to a big meal.

"Hodja, it is doomsday tomorrow. Why don't we all roast your lamb and have one final great meal?" they suggested.

After much effort, they were finally able to convince Nasreddin Hodja to give up his lamb and headed to the river bank for a joyful picnic. First, they put the lamb on the spit to roast. Later they took off their clothes and swam in the river. While everyone was swimming, Nasreddin Hodja collected all of their clothes and threw them in the fire. When they got out of the water they asked him what happened to their clothes.

"What, the clothes? I threw them all in the fire," Nasreddin Hodja said calmly.

"Nasreddin Hodja, why did you do that? What are we supposed to wear now?" asked the youngsters.

"Since tomorrow is doomsday, you won't need your clothes any more," he responded.

6. Jokes about His Economic Situation

Nasreddin Hodja lived in poverty throughout his life. Sometimes he struggled to find even a piece of bread. The problems he had with his wives may have stemmed from his financial situation. The jokes related to financial difficulties reflect both his and his neighbors' situation.

Samples of Jokes

Duck Soup

Nasreddin Hodja had nothing to eat in his house but a small piece of stale bread. So he went for a walk near a lake where ducks were swimming. He began to dip his bread into the lake.

"Nasreddin, what are you doing?" asked a man.

"I am eating duck soup," he replied.

Bread

On a day when Nasreddin Hodja had nothing to eat at home, he passed by a bakery full of bread.

Nasreddin Hodja asked the baker, "Does all the bread belong to you?"

"Yes," responded the baker.

"Why don't you eat it all then," he said.

Getting Used to Hunger

Nasreddin Hodja had become so poor that he had to cut back on the amount of the hay he fed his donkey. Seeing that it did not affect the donkey badly, he kept reducing the amount he fed the donkey. However, one day he went to the barn to feed the donkey, he found the animal dead, and lamented, "Oh, my poor donkey! He was just getting used to hunger!"

A Cup of Soup

One day while Nasreddin Hodja was on his way home he craved soup. He was mumbling, "soup...soup..." Those who happened to hear him started to follow him hoping that he would lead them to a delicious bowl of soup. When they arrived at his house, Nasreddin, as well as all the other people who had been following him asked his wife for soup.

His wife said, "What are you talking about Nasreddin? There is nothing to eat at home."

Upon hearing this, he turned toward the people with an empty bowl of soup in his hand, "If there was soup, I was going to serve it to you in this cup! I am sorry, you are unlucky; we have nothing."

Fight

One day Nasreddin Hodja and his wife were starving as there was nothing to eat at home. Nasreddin Hodja and his wife decided to their neighbors who were preparing dinner at that time. But they had to make up a story about why they were there. Nasreddin came up with a plan and instructed his wife, "You go to their house at dinner time, and I will follow you pretending that I was looking for you. And we will catch them having dinner. Of course, they will have to invite us to eat with them."

His wife agreed to this plot and hurried to the neighbor's house where they were having dinner. She told them, "Nasreddin and I had a fight so I came here."

After a short while, Hodja showed up at the door with a stick in his hand and asked about his wife, "

Have you seen my wife?"

"Yes, but come on in, we were about to have dinner. Let's eat together and then we will help you reconcile," said the neighbor.

As they were dining, the neighbor's brought out a delicious dessert on a round tray. Nasreddin Hodja hadn't had such a dessert in a long time. He ate the portion in front of him but was not satisfied. He started to rotate the tray while scolding his wife at the same time, "When we get home, I am going to pull your ear and twist it just like this."

"Have mercy, Nasreddin! Don't do that!" While the host was trying to pacify Nasreddin Hodja, he was enjoying the dessert that had been on the other side of the tray. When they were both full, Nasreddin Hodja and his wife home holding each other's hands.

7. Jokes about His Congregation

Nasreddin Hodja worked both as a prayer leader (*imam*) and a preacher at various mosques in Akşehir. Therefore, there are plenty of jokes about his congregation. The most notable point in those jokes is his understanding of authentic Islam. He focuses mostly on the ethical principals of the religion and recommends that his congregation follow them. For instance, if a person in his congregation asked a question which does not bear much importance in the daily life of an average Muslim, he aptly diverted their attention from this topic.

In addition, he maintained a balance when talking about this world and the Hereafter. When answering questions on intangible or abstract topics he provided concrete examples from everyday life. Nasreddin Hodja never left a question unanswered. This did not just apply to religious issues; people also consulted him on various mundane issues. He served as a guide who showed people the right path and suggested solutions to the members of his congregation.

Samples of Jokes

Performing Ablutions

One day a person from Nasreddin Hodja's congregation asked, "Which way is a person supposed to face while he is performing the *ghusl* ablution in the lake? (*Ghusl* is a special ablution performed in Islam that requires washing the entire body.)

Hodja replied: "You should face where your clothes are!"

Nasreddin Hodja's Reply

One day a person notorious for asking absurd questions came to Akşehir and asked to see the most knowledgeable person in the city.

People introduced him to Nasreddin Hodja. The man said, "Hodja, I will ask you 40 questions and you have to answer them all at once."

"OK! Ask your questions," he said.

The man asked 40 questions in succession. When he was done with asking the questions, Nasreddin Hodja turned to the man and gave his answer: "I don't know."

The Lie

One day Nasreddin Hodja was delivering a sermon at the mosque. When he saw that some people were yawning and others were half asleep, he changed the topic,

"I was walking outside Akşehir of the village and came across four-footed ducks swimming in the river."

Hearing the phrase "four-footed ducks" was enough to wake people up, and they started to listen carefully. As he looked at them from his raised chair, he said, "You are such strange people. When I was telling the truth, you were asleep. But when I tell an absurd lie, you listen attentively."

What Day of the Month Is It?

While wandering in the marketplace, Nasreddin Hodja came across a man who asked him, "Nasreddin Hodja, what is the date today? Is it the third or fourth of the month?"

"I have no idea. I am not in the moon business," replied Nasreddin Hodja.

8. *Jokes about Lawsuits*

As mentioned in the previous chapters, Nasreddin Hodja worked as a judge (*qadi*) of the city after receiving legal training. This post enabled him to closely observe the societal problems. His jokes reveal both people's vices as well as the corrupt legal system of the time, which included the use of false witnesses and bribes, which grew out of the larger problems in society.

Nasreddin Hodja is featured either as a judge or a defender/litigant in these jokes.

Samples of Jokes

Slap

One day a total stranger randomly slapped Nasreddin Hodja on the cheek. Nasreddin Hodja took him to court, but the defendant had bribed the judge in advance. On the day of the trial the judge ruled, "The penalty for the crime is a silver coin. Let the defendant bring it to you."

Nasreddin Hodja figured out that he had been tricked. After waiting for a while and realizing that the man was not going to come back, he approached the judge and slapped him on the neck. "I can't wait any longer. You can take the coin when he comes back," he said.

The Sound of the Coins

When Hodja was working as a judge, a strange case came before him. The litigant presented his argument, "This guy was cutting down trees in the forest, and I supported him by snapping my fingers to a beat as he hit the tree with his axe. I expect compensation for my service to this man.

After a short while, Hodja asked for the defendant's wallet. The defendant did not understand his intentions and handed it to him. Nasreddin Hodja took the coins and dropped them on a wooden surface to count them. Turning to the defendant, Nasreddin Hodja said, "The fee has been paid."

The man was confused, "What?"

The clinking of the coins is fair compensation for you snapping your fingers, he replied.

9. Jokes about His Neighbors

Nasreddin Hodja had close ties with his neighbors. He interacted with them in the marketplace, on the farm, at wedding ceremonies, at the mosque, and on the street. The essential characteristics of Nasreddin Hodja are evident in his relationships with his neighbors.

Nasreddin Hodja was adept at correcting his neighbors' faults without hurting them. He chose the right time and place to give lessons. His way of being critical yet not disrespectful should be emulated by other intellectuals.

Samples of Jokes

A Cauldron Full of Dessert

One day while Nasreddin Hodja was on his way to home, his friend called out to him, "Nasreddin Hodja, did you see that? Somebody passed by with a cauldron full of dessert."

Nasreddin answered calmly, "It is none of my business."

"But Hodja, the cauldron was headed to your house," continued the man.

"Then it is none of *your* business."

Forty Year-Old Vinegar

One day, a neighbor said to Hodja,

"They say you have vinegar that is forty years old."

"Yes, I do," he replied.

"Can you give me a little?" asked the neighbor.

Nasreddin Hodja replied, "If I gave a little to everybody who asked for it, it would not be forty years old!"

Flour on the Clothesline

A neighbor came to Nasreddin Hodja's door and asked to borrow a clothesline.

"I am sorry, dear friend, but we cannot lend you the clothesline for we have sprinkled flour on it."

"Why would a person sprinkle flour on a clothesline," asked the neighbor in disbelief.

"When one does not want to lend it to someone," replied Nasreddin Hodja.

Visiting the Sick

One day while Nasreddin Hodja was sick andresting in bed his neighbors came to visit him. But they stayed and talked too much and about depressing things.

One day when he was still in bed, one of his neighbors came in, "Nasreddin Hodja, it seems you are terribly sick. We never know when the angel of death will come to take our lives. Have you written your will?"

"Yes, I did," said he replied.

"What did you write? What is your will?" asked the curious neighbor.

Nodding, he responded, "My will is that when you visit the sick, don't stay too long."

Who Do You Believe?

One day, one of Nasreddin Hodja's friends asked if he could borrow his donkey. Hodja, not wanting to lend him his donkey, said, "The donkey is not home."

At that very moment, the donkey started to bray.

His neighbor turned to him angrily and shouted, "Aren't you ashamed of lying to me?"

Nasreddin Hodja, in turn, became very angry and shouted back, "Don't you have any sense? Whom do you believe, me or the donkey?"

10. Nasreddin Hodja as a Guest

Nasreddin Hodja has many jokes related to the many places he visited and events he attended. As the product of a culture where hospitality is valued, he is often seen as either the host or the guest in his jokes. He is invited to feasts, weddings, and various other social events. He was invited to other villages and cities. And of course, many things happened during those visits. Nasreddin Hodja criticized the hosts treated their guests differently based on their style of dress and social status. In addition, he also draws attention of the actions of the more impudent guests.

Samples of Jokes

Honeycomb

One day Nasreddin Hodja visited his neighbor. His neighbor served him and the other guests honey. While each guest tasted a spoonful honeycomb and then stopped eating, Nasreddin Hodja was not satisfied and continued to eat. Honey was expensive and the host warned him with an excuse, "You'd better not eat too much! You might get heartburn."

Hodja replied, "Only God knows whose heart is burning!"

The Neighbor's Head

One day one of the richest men in Akşehir invited Nasreddin Hodja to his home. Nasreddin arrived on time and could see the man's head through the window. He knocked on the door and said, "I am here to see the gentleman of the house."

The man who answered the door informed him that the gentleman was not home.

"Then, please tell him that the next time he goes out he should not leave his head in the window."

The Saddlebag

Nasreddin Hodja lost his saddlebag in the town he was visiting. When he discovered that it was lost, he threatened, "You either find my saddlebag or else! The villagers were alarmed and looked for his bag everywhere. After they finally found it, they returned it to him. Yet the villagers wondered what Nasreddin Hodja would have done if his bag had not been found. He shrugged and said, "I have an old rug at home. I was going to cut it up to make another saddlebag."

The Feast

One day Nasreddin Hodja and a couple of friends decided to spend a few days in a beautiful village and they divided the food preparation among themselves. One of them offered, "I will bring my lamb for the feast."

Another one said, "I will make stuffed eggplant."

While still another person said, "I will make the pastries."

They then turned to Nasreddin Hodja, "Well, what will you do then?" He replied, "I will do my best not to miss such a feast!"

Compote

On a hot summer evening during the Ramadan fast, Hodja was invited for fast breaking dinner. First, they serve the compote with ice. To tease the guests, the host began to eat the compote with a big soup ladle and each time he took a sip from the iced compote, he said:

Oh! I could die. Hodja and other guests tried to drink compote with small spoons they were given and could not even taste it. When others kept slient, Hodja could not restrain himself and looked at the host:

- Would you give me your soup ladle and let me die a little too?

11. Jokes about Timur

There are a number of jokes about Timur and Nasreddin Hodja. However, while it is now clear that these jokes do not actually belong to Nasreddin Hodja, it is important to understand that in these jokes Timur represents all authority figures and is the symbol of oppression. People made up these stories as a way to react to the oppression. At that time, the local governor of Akşehir was also an oppressive ruler. It is possible that these jokes were originally written about this ruler and his name was replaced with Timur's over time.

In these jokes, Nasreddin Hodja courageously stands in strong opposition to Timur. He was blunt and honest. However, when Timur was angry, Nasreddin tried to pacify him through song and wit.

Samples of Jokes

One day Nasreddin Hodja was in the presence of Timur when Timur's men brought in a soldier who was very drunk. They asked Timur how he should be punished.

"Hit him three hundred times with a cane!" ordered Timur. Upon hearing this harsh sentence, Nasreddin Hodja burst into laughter.

"Hodja, Hodja! How dare you laugh?" Timur thundered, "What is so funny? Are you making fun of me?"

"God forbid, Great Timur. I am not making fun of you." Nasreddin explained, "I laugh because you either have never been beaten with a cane or you do not know how to count."

Nasreddin Hodja's Old Ox

One day Timur invited Nasreddin Hodja to play the javelin on horses. Nasreddin arrived at the field riding an ox.

Timur asked, "Nasreddin Hodja! What is this? The javelin is played with agile animals like horses. Why did you bring this old ox?"

Hodja answered, "Oh Timur! You should have seen this ox when it was a calf. It was so agile that not even a bird could have caught it."

The Most Courageous Man

One day Timur told the people of Akşehir, "Bring the most courageous man amongst you. I will assign a very important task to him."

But nobody dared to approach Timur. Then, they decided put forward Nasreddin Hodja as the bravest man in town. They told Nasreddin, "No one other than you could accomplish this. Please agree to meet Timur."

Unwilling to let the people down, he agreed to see Timur. Timur challenged him, "Let's see how courageous you are!"

He asked Nasreddin to stand in a square in front of a tree. He then ordered his archer to aim at Nasreddin. The arrow went through Nasreddin Hodja's legs and hit the tree. Another arrow passed right under his armpit. The last one hit his turban. Seeing that Nasreddin Hodja stood still, Timur praised him, "I appreciate your courage, Nasreddin. You've proven that you are a brave man."

He then ordered his soldiers to bring a new robe and a turban him as his turban and robe had been ripped by the arrows.

Nasreddin Hodja shyly said, "Please tell them to bring underwear for me too!"

Teaching the Donkey

One day Nasreddin Hodja said to Timur, "If you give me three years time and 3000 gold coins, I can teach my donkey how to read." Nasreddin's friends who had witnessed his proposition were concerned and cautioned him, "If you are unable to teach the donkey how to read in three years time, Timur will kill you."

Nasreddin Hodja replied calmly "My dear friends! In three years time, either the donkey or Timur will die. If none of them dies, then it means that I will die!"

Nasreddin Hodja's Old Donkey

Nasreddin Hodja's donkey got so old that it was of no use to him anymore. Therefore, one day he let the old donkey go in the mountains and bought a new one.

A few days later, while hunting on the mountain Timur saw the poor old donkey. He felt sorry for it and ordered his men to find which cruel person had left the donkey there to die. When they returned with Nasreddin Hodja, Timur rebuked him: "You are such an ungrateful person. You kept your donkey while he was beneficial to you, and when he got older, you wanted to get rid of the poor animal. Now, take him home with you and take good care of him! I will send one of my men to check upon the donkey from time to time. So, you better watch your steps! If you do not follow my orders, I will kill you!"Nasreddin took the donkey home and took care of him. After a short while, the donkey had grown stronger and was rejuvenated. As he was braying happily, Nasreddin

Hodja murmured, "You can bray as much as you like! After all, you have a guardian like Timur."

B. In Verse

The original jokes of Nasreddin Hodja are written in prose. However, they can also be found written in verse. When written in verse his jokes not only appeal to those who prefer to read in verse, but they are also easier to remember.

Some earliest examples of Nasreddin Hodja's jokes in verse are found in the works of the poets Güvahi and Taşlıcalı Yahya Bey, who lived during the rule of Süleyman the Magnificent in the 16th century, and Nevizade Atai in the 17th century. However, only a small number of Nasreddin Hodja's jokes were written in verse during this time period.

Çaylak Tevfik, Ateşzade Mehmet İzzet Paşa, and Ali Ekrem Bolayır also wrote Hodja's jokes as verse.

Mehmet Fuat Köprülü first published the jokes written in verse as a book. This book, published in 1918, consists of 50 jokes written in verse. Thirty years later, Orhan Veli Kanık published another book consisting of 70 of Nasreddin Hodja's jokes in verse form. The works of Abdullah Rıza Ergüven, Orhan Seyfi Orhon, Fazıl Hüsnü Dağlarca, Tahir Abacı, İbrahim Zeki Burdurlu, Ömür Candaş, Sadi Cumbul, Sami Ergun, İbrahim Güleç, Kemal Özer, Nejat Sefercioğlu, Yusuf Ahıskalı, Vahap Tuncer, Hasan Latif Sarıyüce, Tekin Sönmez, Vahap Tuncer, H. Zekai Yiğitler, Bestami Yazgan, Ali Püsküllüoğlu, Hâlistin Kukul, and A. Vahap Akbaş followed in the twentieth century.

Some examples of Nasreddin Hodja's jokes in verse

Kadı ile Nasreddin Hoca

Var idi Konya'da bir kadı-i şum,
İrtişa vü tama ile mezmum.

Ana her kim ki verirdi rüşvet
Muktezasınca yazardı hüccet

Hace-i devr-i zaman Nasraddin
Eyledi kadıya bir hile hemin:

Koydu bir testiye vafir toprak,
Kadıyı aldadı ol salik-i hak.

Bir kaşık bal koyup ağzına heman
Toprağı eyledi testide nihan.

Haceti olmuş idi bir hüccet,
Kadıya testiyi verdi rüşvet.

Hürmet etti ana kadı, durdu,
Rüşveti gördü, safalar sürdü.

Kalemin aldı eline kadı,
Hücceti yazmağa oldu razı.

Eyledi sây-i belîği ikdam,
Haceti eyledi yanında tamam.

Hücceti verdi edip kat'ı niza,
Kadıya eyledi ol dahi veda.

Yemeğe başladı kadı aseli,
Toprağa erdi kaza ile eli.

Kadıya oldu kaziye malum,
Gönlüne kibr ü gazap etti hücum.

Gördü anı, nitekim ehl-i riya:
Zâhiri batına uymaz kat'a.

Testiyi hışm ile ol kadı-i mest
Kalb-i uşşak gibi kıldı şikest.

Kadı bir hile vü tezvir etti.
Hücceti almağa tebdil etti.

Eyleyip dilde nihan-ı kine
Derdi yarındası Nasruddin'e:

— Getir ol hücceti kim yanlışı var,
Bir dahisini yazayım tekrar.

Yanlış olunca keşide hüccet
Kendi davasına vermez suret...

Dinleyince bu sözü Nasruddin
Söyledi kadıya lûtf ile hemin:

— Hüccetin cümle sahih, ey nâdân!
Var ise testidedir yanlış olan...

Rüşvet ile yaşayan ahmaktır,
Anı bilmez ki sonu topraktır.

Versified by: Taşlıcalı Yahya[100]

The Judge and Nasreddin Hoca

There was a corrupt judge in Konya
Notorious for bribery and avarice

Whoever bribed this judge
Would get the appropriate verdict

The great Nasreddin Hodja
Plotted against the judge:

Stuffed an earthenware jug with sand,
The follower of truth entrapped the corrupt judge.

Putting a spoonful of honey in his mouth,
He concealed the sand inside the jug.

His petition was accepted
Bribing the judge with the jug

---

[100] Taşlıcalı Yahya Bey was a 16th century classical Ottoman poet. He was a prominent *ghazel* (ode) poet. He put this particular joke of Nasreddin Hodja in his book *Gencine-i Râz*.

The judge respected Nasreddin
Seeing the bribe, revered Nasreddin.

He took the pen in his hand
Started to write the court decision in favor of Nasreddin

Nasreddin Hodja delivered an eloquent speech
And got the court decision at last

The court decision ended the dispute
And he said goodbye to the judge

The judge started to eat the honey from the jug
His hand suddenly reached the sand

When the judge figured out what was going on,
His heart was filled with great wrath.

The hypocrite saw the sand in the jug
Saw the appearance did not resonate with the unseen.

The deceived judge was angry with Nasreddin
He was defeated like a lover.

He plotted a hoax against him.
He wanted to get the decision back from him.

Concealing his feelings of revenge
The judge informed Nasreddin Hodja:

"There was something wrong with the decree,
I will correct it if you bring it back to me."

Pretending to focus on the mistake on the written decree,
He did not mention the issue of honey.

Hearing the judge's concern
Hodja responded calmly:

"The decree was all correct, ignorant judge!
There must be something wrong with the jug."

The person who lives on bribery is a fool.
He tends to forget the reckoning in the grave.

Hoca ile eşeği

Bizim Hoca eşeğinden
Hiç inmez, binicidir
Lâkin bazı koştururken
Düşer, kendini incitir.
Birgün şehrin meydanında
Süvarilik aşkı coşar
Ciridi varmış yanında;
Bir kahraman gibi koşar.
Lâkin çok sürmez bu koşma,
Hoca birden yere düşer.
Yerinden kalkmadan daha
Başına çocuklar üşer:

"Hoca, biz dedikti sana.
Neye bu kadar koşturdun?
Bak süvarilik satana!
Hocam, neye böyle durdun?"

Türlü lâflar söyleyerek
Hepsi geldi bir kulp taktı.
Hoca gördü ki boş emek,
Cevap vermeyerek baktı.
En sonunda herkes sustu
Hoca ne diyecek? diye.
Hoca mağrur bir tavustu,
Toz kondurmadı beyliğe.

İlerledi yavaş yavaş,
Dedi: "Yok mu başka derdim?
Neye iyi bunca telaş?
Düşmeseydim inecektim…"[101]

Versified by: M. Fuat Köprülü

Hodja and His Donkey

Nasreddin Hodja does not
Dismount his donkey, a rider is he.
But sometimes rearing the donkey
He falls off, and gets hurt.
In the town square one day
Acting like a cavalier
Holding his javelin in his hand
Riding like a hero.
His showing-off does not take long
He fell to the ground
Before he could get up
Kids flocked around:

"Didn't we tell you Nasreddin?
Why did you show-off like that?
See what happens to fake cavaliers.
Why did you stop now?

Accusing Nasreddin,
They found him guilty.
Seeing that it was pointless
Did not bother to answer him
Everyone calmed down
To listen what he had to say.
Nasreddin Hodja was a haughty peacock

---

[101] M. Fuat Köprülü, *Nasreddin Hoca*, p. 160-162

Not letting them belittle him
Moved forward slowly and said:
"Why are you so concerned?
Don't you have any other problems?
I would have gotten off it anyway
Had I not fallen off."[102]

Yorgan Kavgası

Bir gece, Hoca yatakta
Rahat rahat uyuyorken;
Bir gürültü, bir şamata
Koptu da kapıda birden.
Buna dayanamazdı insan;
Hoca fırladı yataktan!
Pencereyi açıp baktı:
Lâkin karanlıktı sokak,
Karısı şamdanı yaktı,
Korkudan kalbi vurarak:
— Aman bakma pencereden!
Hem buna karışmak neden?

Fakat Hoca pek meraklı;
Fazla söz dinleyemezdi...
Kavgada kalmıştı aklı:
Deminki ses nasıl sesti?
Devam ederken harıltı
Hoca fazla duramadı!

Başındaki takiyyesini
Düzeltip yorganı aldı;
Karısı artık, sesini
Çıkarmayıp bakakaldı.

102 M. Fuat Köprülü, ibid., p.160-162.

Arkasından bir şal yorgan,
Hoca fırladı kapıdan...

— Yahu nedir gürültünüz
Gece vakti böyle sizin?
Torbaya mı girdi gündüz?
Artık yeter, sesi kesin!
Hem bilelim, nedir dava,
Kör dövüşü yetmez mi ya?

Hepsi boş gürültü müthiş,
Hoca'nın sözü kaynadı;
Derken karanlıkta; ne iş!
Yorgan arada oynadı.
Çırılçıplak kaldı Hoca,
Çekildi hemen bir uca...

Gürültü çoğalmıştı pek!
Baktı Hoca, biraz kalsa
Don gömlek bile gidecek...
Hemen: "Bende akıl olsa
Yatağımdan çıkar mıydım?"
Deyip döndü nadim nadim.

Bu esnada, dışarıdaki
Gürültüler hep kesildi;
En sonra kalan bir iki
Ayak sesi de kesildi;
Ne gürültü ne patırtı
Hoca buna şaşakaldı!

Şaşkın şaşkın giriyorken
Odaya karısı sordu:
"Kavga ne imiş? Böyle birden,
Neye uzamayıp durdu?
Sanıyordum uzayacak,
Sabaha sürecek mutlak?"

Hoca, biraz düşünerek
Durdu başını salladı;
Anlamıştı bu sırrı pek,
Damağında vardı tadı,
Dedi: "Bizim yorgan gitti,
O gidince, dava bitti..."[103]

Versified by: M. Fuat Köprülü

The Quilt is Gone

One night when Nasreddin Hodja was in bed
Sleeping like a baby;
He suddenly heard
A hubbub and rumble
One could not resist such clamor
So Nasreddin leaped out of bed,
Opened the windows and looked around
Too dark was the street to see
His wife lit a candle,
Of course, her heart throbbing in fear

"Do not look outside the window!
Why are you meddling?"

Yet Nasreddin, so curious,
Could not listen to what she said.
Thinking of the fight outside:
Such a rumble it was!
As the noise kept on
Nothing could stop him!

Wearing his skullcap
Wrapped in his warm quilt;
His wife kept silent

---

[103] M. Fuat Köprülü, ibid., p. 83-85

Watched him in bewilderment.
The quilt on his shoulders,
Nasreddin left his home.

"Why are you making noise
In the middle of the night?
What happened to the days?
Stop fighting! That's enough!
Tell me why you fight,
What is this brawl for?"

There was nothing but much crying and a little wool
His words had gone unnoticed
Suddenly, something happened!
The quilt just disappeared.
Nasreddin Hodja was left naked,
Forsaking the hustle and bustle of the fight.

Yet the noise just increased!
Understanding that if he stayed longer
He would lose the underwear.
He said to himself: "If I were a wise man
I would not have left my bed"
And returned to the home in repentance.

All the noise outside
Disappeared at once;
Even the last footsteps
Faded away immediately;
Neither the fight nor the noise could be heard
Nasreddin was shocked!

As he entered the room
His wife asked him:
"What was the fight about?
Why did it come to a halt?
I thought it would go on
Til morning."

Pondering for a second
Shaking his head;
He got the point now,
Felt its bitter taste,
and said: "The quilt is gone,
And the fight is over."[104]

Kavuk

Birgün bir adam, elinde mektup,
Der ki Hoca'yı tutup:
"Hocam, zahmet ya, sana,
Şu mektubu bir okusana!"

Açar bakar ki Hoca,
Mektup baştan sona Arapça.
Şöyle bir evirir, çevirir;
Söktüremez çaresiz geri verir.
Der ki: "Başkasına okut bunu sen."
Adam, şaşırır: "Neden?"
"Türkçe değil, bu mektup okuyamam."
Yine anlamaz adam.
Hoca'nın okuması yok zanneder.
"Ayıp, Hoca! Ayıp." der.
"Benden utanmıyorsun, şundan utan!
Şu başındaki koca kavuğundan."
Hoca, kavuğu çıkarıp uzatır.
Sonra da: "Mademki der, iş kavuktadır;
Haydi, benim düdüğüm, giy de şunu
Kendin oku bakalım mektubunu."[105]

Versified by: O. Veli Kanık

---

[104] M. Fuat Köprülü, ibid., p. 83-85.
[105] O. Veli Kanık, *Nasreddin Hoca Hikâyeleri*, p. 34

Turban

One day a man with a letter in his hand
Asked Nasreddin Hodja,
"I don't want to bother you,
But, could you read this letter for me?"

Hodja opened it only to see
The letter was in Arabic.
Taking a look at it again;
He did not see a single word and
Told the man, "Take this letter to somebody else."
The man asked in puzzlement, "Why?"
"I cannot read it, it's not in Turkish."
The man did not understand.
He thought Nasreddin did not know how to read.
"Shame on you, Nasreddin Hodja!" he said.
"You are wearing the turban of a learned man
But you don't know how to read.
Be ashamed of your turban!"
Nasreddin took off his turban.
Placed it in front of the man.
"If it is still a turban
Put it on, and read your letter!"[106]

Eşeğe danışayım

Saygısız bir komşusu
Eşeğe kurup pusu
Rahmetlinin evine
Erkenden koşar yine:
"Komşular yardım sever
Eşeğini biraz ver"
Hoca ise yanaşmaz

---

[106] O. Veli Kanık, ibid., p. 34.

Der ki: "Sen bana biraz
Müsaade et de bayım
Eşeğe bir danışayım
Fikrini bir alayım."
"Peki" derse eşeğim
Alıp gitmekte hürsün
Sağlıkla götürürsün.

Hoca az sonra gelir
Komşusuna yönelir:
"Gider misin?" deyince
Sızlandı ince ince
Sonra dedi ki: "Hayır"
Üstelik göğsü şişti
Şu ricaya girişti:
"Belâdan beni kayır
Verirsen yabancıya
Bakmaz sızı acıya
Beni dürtükler, döver
Sırtıma bir çul takılmaz;
Seni de boş bırakmaz,
Yedi ceddine söver."[107]

Versified by: Sami Ergun

Let Me Ask My Donkey

A rude neighbor of Nasreddin Hodja's
Coveting his donkey
Rushed to his house again,
"Neighbors help each other out.
Lend me your donkey today."
He was reluctant to do so

---

[107] Sami Ergun, *Manzum Nasreddin Hoca Fıkraları ve Hikâyeleri*, p. 70

He told the man,
"Give me a few seconds
I will ask my donkey
If he is willing to go with you.
If he agrees to do so,
You are free to take him."

Nasreddin came back alone
Turned to his neighbor and said,
"When I asked if he wanted to go,
The donkey moaned unwillingly.
And then he said, "No."
Then, my donkey took a deep sigh
And asked me a favor,
"Protect me from trouble.
If you give me to a stranger and
He beats me to death
He will not forget you
He will swear at you too!"[108]

Eşeğe yeşil gözlük

Hoca merhum bir zaman
Ot bulamadığından
Eşeğine durmadan
Yediriyormuş geven

Hep geven yiyen hayvan
Usanmış tatlı canından
Açlığa katlanır olmuş
Yemez olmuş gevenden

Otu nerde bulsun Hoca
Düşünmüş buna çare

---

[108] Sami Ergun, ibid., p. 70.

Yeşil camdan gözlük yapmış
Eşeğin gözüne göre

Eşek yeşil gözlükten
Geveni ot sanınca
Girişmiş iştahla ot yemeye
"Seni köftehor, demiş Hoca
Dört ayaküstüne düştun yine."[109]

Versified by: Sabutay H. Karahasanoğlu

Green Glasses for the Donkey

When Nasreddin Hodja was very poor
When he could not find green grass for his donkey
He fed his donkey wild liquorice.

Fed up with eating the liquorice
The donkey was so upset
It was better not to eat at all
Than to keep eating liquorice

Where could he find green grass?
Nasreddin searched for a solution
He made a pair of glasses with green glass
That would fit over the donkey's eyes

After putting on the green glasses
Believing that the liquorice was green grass
The donkey devoured it.
Seeing his donkey enjoying its food
Hodja mocked it,
"You lucky donkey!
You landed on your feet."[110]

---

[109] S. Hikmet Karahasanoğlu, *Nasreddin Hoca*, p. 49
[110] Ibid., p. 49.

Tabutun içinde bulunma da

Yine bir gün komşudan
Biri vefat etmişti.
Herkes işi gücü bırakıp
Cenazeye gitmişti.

O sırada bir adam,
Yaklaşmış Nasreddin'e.
Demiş: "Sorum olacak,
Ey Hocam sana yine.

Acımız fazla büyük,
Elbette sabretmeli!
Cenaze götürürken,
Neresinden gitmeli?"

Hoca demiş: "Elbette,
Sonu budur her kulun!
Tabutta bulunma da
Nerde istersen bulun!"

Versified by: Hâlistin Kukul

It doesn't Matter

Another one of Nasreddin Hodja's neighbors
Passed away one day.
Everyone was waiting
At the funeral of the neighbor.

Someone among the people
Approached Nasreddin
The man told him,
"I got a question for you."

"Our sorrow is great today,
Of course, we will be patient!

While carrying the coffin,
Where should the mourners should stand?"

Nasreddin Hodja responded:
"Of course, we will all go there one day.
For now as long as you are not the one inside,
It does not matter where you stand."

Anası ağlayacak

Yakınlarda bir köyde, Hoca'nın büyük oğlu,
Çömlekçilik yaparmış; bu imiş geçim yolu.
Hoca, birgün oğlunu ziyarete gidince,
Oğlan saygı göstermiş, elinden geldiğince.
Çalıştığı yere de yürümüşler beraber;
Ipıslak çömleklerle doluymuş hemen her yer.
"Bak baba!" demiş oğlan, "Bütün paralarımı,
Çömleklere yatırdım; seyret artık kârımı!
Hava güneşli olur da hepsi kurursa elbet;
Ama hani olur ya, yağmur yağarsa şayet,
İşte baba, o zaman, bilesin anam ağlar!"

Hoca, ordan ayrılır, küçük oğluna uğrar.
O da lâf arasında demiş ki babasına:
"Varım yoğum şu tarla; çok emek verdim ona.
İyi bir yağmur yağsa, zengin oldum gitti bil;
Ama kuraklık olsa, olacağım sersefil!
Yağmazsa anam ağlar, baba, bilesin bunu!"

Hoca, canı pek sıkkın, tutmuş evin yolunu.
"Ah efendi, bu ne hâl?" demiş ona karısı:
"Ne oldu sana böyle, yüzün çifit çarşısı!"
"Benimki bir şey mi ki... Asıl kendini düşün;
İki oğlan anası, oldukça zordur işin!

Yağmur boşansa şayet, ağlayacaksın kesin;
Yağmasa, ağlayacak olan da yine sensin!"

Versified by: A. Vahap Akbaş

Mom Will Cry

Nasreddin Hodja's elder son lived in a nearby village.
He sold pottery, that was his bread and butter.
When Nasreddin visited his son one day
He welcomed his father.
They walked to his son's shop.
The place was fraught with wet pottery.
"Look, Dad!" said the son, "I spent all my money,
On this pottery: we will see my profit!
If it will be sunny and they will all dry up.
But if it happens to rain,
My mom will cry!"

Hodja left to call on his younger son.
The younger son too complained,
"All I have is this farm, I spent all my fortune on it.
If it rains a lot, I will become rich;
Should there be drought, my mom will cry!"

Nasreddin Hodja returned home bored.
"What happened, Hodja?" asked his wife,
"Why are you so sullen today?"
"That's not important! You'd better think of your own situation.
It is hard to be the mother of two sons.
It does not matter whether or not it rains.
You are going to cry anyway!"

C. FROM A SUFI PERSPECTIVE

Burhaneddin Çelebi, who commented on 121 of Nasreddin Hodja's jokes, is one of the most prominent scholars who interpreted his jokes from a Sufi perspective. Burhaneddin Çelebi makes the following comment about Nasreddin Hodja, "The great Nasreddin Hodja, may he rest in peace, was a man of humor who is known to have been among the dignitaries of his time."

Nasreddin Hodja gave his messages in a humorous way; nevertheless, it is misleading to assume that his intention was only to entertain people. The jokes should be more deeply analyzed in order to understand the wit and invaluable advice they give. Like Rumi pointed out in this couplet:

Our *bayit* (couplet) is not a *bayt* (house) but a country
Our mockery is not a mockery but a lesson.

In fact, this metaphor is succinct and the mockery teaches a lesson. Since the meaning is only implied, the analysis of Hodja's jokes from a Sufi perspective could prove fruitful.[111] The same approach has also been embraced by two contemporary poets Ali Günvar and Şaban Abak.[112-113]

Nasreddin Hodja's Jokes From a Sufi Perspective

Winged camel

One day Nasreddin Hodja said to the people,

"Praise God for creating camels without wings. Had they had wings, they would have demolished our houses and destroyed our gardens."

Comment

Do not take for granted the greatness and blessings of God. Express gratitude even if you have not been bestowed with prestige, high rank and abundant property. For everybody receives as much as they

---

[111] *Letaif-i Nasreddin Hoca*, Fikret Türkmen.

[112] Ali Günvar, *Yedi İklim* dergisi, ibid., p. 9-11.

[113] See Ali Günvar and Şaban Abak's articles in *Yedi İklim* dergisi issue 138-139 for more examples of these comments, Burhaneddin Çelebi's work referenced in the bibliography, and the İsmailEmre.net website.

can handle. Should one lack the skill to handle what has been bestowed upon him, he would resemble a winged camel. Not only would he be at risk for sin, he could also lead others to wrongdoing.

The Dead Wandering Around

One day while Nasreddin Hodja was wandering around in the countryside, he ran into a few men on horses. After he saw the men, he took off his clothes and hid in a grave. The cavaliers came up and said, "You crazy man! Why are you lying here?"

"I am a dead man and this is my grave. I went out for a walk," he responded.

Comment

This world is an arable field for the Hereafter. Die (in terms of your carnal self) before your real death, take off the garments of pride and put on the cerement (remembering death saves you from worldliness). Prepare your provisions for the journey to the other world. Sooner or later, death will come one day.

D. JOKES IN DIFFERENT COUNTRIES

Doom's Day (Uighur)

One of the dignitaries invited Nasreddin Hodja to his home to ask the following question:

"Hodja! You are known to be one of the most learned men of our time. So, tell me about the end of the world. When will it come to an end?"

"The day after you pass away," responded Nasreddin.

"How do you know that?" continued the perplexed man.

"The moment you die, your heirs will turn the world upside down to get the lion's share from your fortune," was Nasreddin's response.

Butcher and Surgeon (Uzbek)

One day Nasreddin Hodja was asked the following:

"Nasreddin Hodja, are a butcher and a surgeon different?"

"Of course, they are different," Nasreddin Hodja replied.

"How are they different?" asked the people.

"The butcher kills first and then skins the animals whereas a surgeons skins something first and kills it later," responded Nasreddin.

The Cat and the Meat (Azeri)

Molla Nasreddin brought three kilograms of meat home and asked his wife to cook it for dinner. However, the wife served okra instead at dinner.

Nasreddin Hodja asked:

"What happened to the meat?"

"Don't ask! The cat took it and fled!"

At that time, the cat was in the room. Hodja caught it, fetched the scale, and weighed the cat. Then he said, "The cat weighs exactly three kilograms, and I bought three kilograms of meat. Now tell me, if this is the cat, where is the meat? Or, if that is the meat, where is the cat?"

Vine Shoots (Turkmen)

Effendi (Nasreddin Hodja) was planting vine shoots in a row. A friend of him, who was watching him, asked, "When will they grow and when will you be able to harvest them? It is not likely that you are going to taste those grapes."

"You are right! We have eaten what the others planted, and others should eat from what we have sown."

How Many Buddies Do You Have? (Kazakh)

When Nasreddin Hodja was a judge, people asked him, "Do you have a lot of friends?"

"I have too many friends to count now. But I will know the real number when I step down from this post."

The Fortune Teller (Persian)

One day a man came up to Nasreddin Hodja and told him that he was a fortune teller.

Nasreddin Hodja asked the man, "Ok. What is the name of your next door neighbor?"

"I don't know," said the man.

"If you do not know the name of your next door neighbor, how do you know what the stars signify?"

Coffee (Greek)

One day Nasreddin Hodja went to a coffee shop. As a joke, the owner of the coffee shop placed a piece of paper under the coffee cup. He wrote the following on the paper: "Nasreddin Hodja, the coffee comes all the way from Yemen. It is not enough to pay 20 drachmas (currency of Greece). You should pay 25 drachmas.

Hodja turned over paper and wrote the following: "The coffee comes from Yemen, from such a remote place. If 20 drachmas is not enough, you should close this place."

Fresh Air (Bosnian)

One day Nasreddin Hodja was taking a walk outside the city. He ran into a few men on horseback carrying guns. Nasreddin took off his robe and hid inside a nearby grave.

However, he did not go unnoticed. The cavaliers saw him jump into the grave and asked him, "What are you doing in there?"

"I am one of the dead people here. I was out to get some fresh air," he responded.

APPENDIX

DOCUMENTARY EVIDENCE ABOUT NASREDDIN HODJA

A. WRITTEN DOCUMENTS

The most reliable sources about Nasreddin Hodja are written documents. The following are the most important of them:

a) Mecmua-i Maarif

Mecmua-i Maarif (Journal of Education), first published in 1861 and based on the court records of Hasan Efendi, the *mufti* of Sivrihisar, is the most trusted source on Nasreddin Hodja. Information about Nasreddin's birthdate and place of birth, the places he lived, and the date he passed away as well as the description of his personality are based on this source.[114]

b) Saltukname

Saltukname is a book Ebu'l Hayr Rumi presented to Sultan Mehmed the Conqueror's son, Cem Sultan, as a gift in 1480. It consists of anecdotes of Sarı Saltuk as well as religious and folk stories compiled in Asia Minor and the Balkans. The book also provides information about Nasreddin Hodja's life, personality, jokes, and Sarı Saltuk's visit with Nasreddin Hodja in Sivrihisar.[115]

---

[114] M. Fuat Köprülü, *Nasreddin Hoca* p. 22.

[115] Mustafa Duman, Nasreddin Hoca, *Yedi İklim* dergisi, Nasreddin Hoca Özel Sayısı p. 25.

c) Letaifname

Letaifname is the posthumously published work of Lamii Çelebi (1472-1527), and was completed by his son Abdullah Çelebi. This book too is about Nasreddin Hodja and includes his jokes.[116]

d) Seyahatname (The Book of Travels)

Evliya Çelebi stops by Akşehir, and visits Nasreddin Hodja's tomb. There is a section in this book, which describes Evliya Çelebi's trip to Akşehir where he visits Nasreddin Hodja's tomb, that recounts this visit and t Nasreddin's personality.[117]

e) Kitâb-ı Mir'at-ı Cihan

In this book, written in 1581 by Osman of Bayburt, Nasreddin Hodja is referred as a saintly person."[118]

f) Poets that refer to Nasreddin Hodja's jokes in their work

In his book titled *Budalaname*, Kaygusuz Abdal refers to one of Nasreddin's jokes.[119] References to his jokes are found in the works of other poets too, such as the work of the classical Ottoman poet, Nabi, in 17th century; the minstrels Refiki and Seyrani in the 19th century, and the 20th century poet Hudai.

g) Books on Nasreddin Hodja

The books and articles of Turkish scholars such as Şemsettin Sami, Bursalı Mehmet Tahir, Çaylak Çelebi, Veled Çelebi, Fuad Köprülü,

---

[116] M. Fuat Köprülü, *Nasreddin Hoca* p. 21, Mustafa Kutlu, Nasreddin Hoca, *Türk Edebiyatı*, issue 255 p. 8.

[117] Evliya Çelebi, *Seyahatname*, vol. 3, p. 16.

[118] G. Tarıman Canikoğlu, *Nazım Diliyle Nasreddin Hoca Fıkraları*, Konya'da Kültür ve Sanat, p.126.

[119] Canikoğlu, ibid., p. 126.

İsmail Hami Danişmend, İbrahim Hakkı Konyalı, Abdülbaki Gölpınarlı, Pertev Naili Boratav, Şükrü Kurgan, Ahmet Kutsi Tecer, Şükrü Elçin, Mehmet Önder, Saim Sakaoğlu, Fikret Türkmen, M. Sabri Koz, and Mustafa Duman and foreign scholars like Tahmasıp Ferzeliyev (Azeri), B. Adambayef (Kazakh), Mihail Guboğlu (Gagauz), Nimetullah Hafız (Yugoslavian) Veliçko Valcev (Bulgarian), Masao Mori (Japanese), Dieter Glade (German), Jean-Paul Garnier (French) and Warran Walker (American) are some of the major written sources on Nasreddin Hodja.[120]

B. GRAVESTONE EPITAPHS

a) The gravestone of Nasreddin Hodja's daughter Fatma used to be in the old graveyard in Sivrihisar. It was moved to the Mevlana Museum in Konya and then to the Akşehir Museum.[121]

b) Another gravestone, belonging to Nasreddin Hodja's other daughter Dürri Melek Hatun, abuts his tomb.[122]

c) The gravestones of some people that are thought to be Nasreddin Hodja's relatives who lived in Istanbul in the 13th and 14th centuries such as those of Kasim Efendi (d. 1793) and his daughters, Fatma Zehra (d. 1794) and Hatice (d. 1803).[123]

d) The gravestone of one of Nasreddin Hodja's wives, Habibe (daughter of Mehmet Çelebi).[124]

e) Nasreddin Hodja's tomb and gravestone, which have been authenticated as his, are in Akşehir.[125]

---

[120] M. Sri Koz, *Yedi İklim* dergisi, ibid., p. 43-51, Canikoğlu, ibid., p. 20.

[121] *Yeni Türk Ansiklopedisi* v. 7 p. 2600.

[122] *Yeni Türk Ansiklopedisi* v. 7 p.2600.

[123] Kemal Uzun, a.g. p. 14.

[124] *Yeni Türk Ansiklopedisi* vol.7 p.2600.

[125] M. Fuat Köprülü, *Nasreddin Hoca*, p.23.

C. FOUNDATION RECORDS

a) Nasreddin Hodja's signature as a co-signer was found on the bills (dated 1257 and 1266) of a foundation established by Seyyid Mahmud Hayrani and Hacı İbrahim Sultan in Akşehir.[126]

b) A foundation was established by Nasreddin Hodja himself in Akşehir.[127] According to Document No. 556 in the archives of the Office of Prime Ministry, it has been documented in the records of foundations and real estate, which were prepared by one of the viziers of Sultan Mehmet II, Gedik Ahmet Pasa, that Nasreddin owned a foundation.[128]

c) Information on Nasreddin's tomb and *madrasa* (Muslim theological school) were kept in the city records under Sultan Mehmet II's rule.[129]

D. FAMILY LINEAGE

a) The first *qadi* (judge) and governor of Istanbul and the master of Sultan Mehmet II, Hizir Bey, descended from the same family as Nasreddin Hodja.[130] The father of Hizir Bey, *qadi* (judge) Celaleddin is the son of his daughter Fatma.

---

[126] M. Fuat Köprülü, *Nasreddin Hoca*, p. 22.

[127] İ. Hakkı Konyalı, *Akşehir, Nasreddin Hoca'nın Şehri*, p.460–462.

[128] Mustafa Duman, *Yedi İklim*, a.g. p. 25.

[129] İ. Hakkı Konyalı, ibid., p. 460–461.

[130] Hızır Bey is the son of Celaleddin Emin Arif, a *madrasa* professor and the judge of Ordu and Sivrihisar,, who is Nasreddin Hodja's grandson. Hizir Bey was born on August 6, 1407. After first being trained by his father, he then studied positive and religious education in the Bursa *madrasa* as a student of *Molla* Yegan. His success in debating Arab scholars attracted Sultan Mehmet II's attention, and he was appointed as the first judge and governor or Istanbul soon after Istanbul was conquered. He had two dauthers and three sons; his sons were Sinan Pasha, Molla Yakup Pasha, and Mufti Ahmet Pasha. He wrote several books in Arabic, Persian and Turkish. His most renowned work is *Kaside-i Nuniye*, a 105 couplet encomium. His tomb is in the courtyard of Fatih Mosque in Istanbul.

Judge Celaleddin passed away and was buried in Akşehir when Nasreddin Hodja was the judge Akşehir there.

b) The author of the book titled *Tazarruname*, Sinan Pasha, is the other son of Hizir Bey mentioned above and was born in Sivrihisar.[131]

c) Some individuals in a village called Hortu, meaning "Nasreddin Hodja," claimed to be his relatives.[132]

d) Remnants of a house in the village called Hortu (Nasreddin Hodja) are believed to have belonged to Nasreddin Hodja.[133]

---

[131] Sinan Pasha is the son of the first judge and governor of Istanbul, Hızır Bey. He was born in Sivrihisar in 1427. He was also a student of his father and completed his studies at a young age. As he had the opportunity to get to know his father's friends who were scholars, Sinan Pasha took math and astronomics courses from Ali Kuşçu, the prominent math scholar. He was well trained in both the positive and religious fields. After teaching at various *madrasa*s, he was appointed as a vizier. Due to the smear campaign against him by some scholars, he was expelled to Sivrihisar. With his friend *Molla* Lütfi of Tokat, he established a library in Sivrihisar. Sultan Bayezid II, who followed Mehmet II, reappointed Sinan Pasha as a vizier and a professor at the *madrasa* in Edirne. He was buried in Edirne. His most renowned book is *Tazarruname*.

[132] Mustafa Kutlu, Nasreddin Hoca, *Türk Edebiyatı* [Journal of Turkish Literature] issue 255 p. 8, Şükrü Kurgan, Nasreddin Hoca, p. 17.

[133] *Türk Dili ve Edebiyatı Ansiklopedisi* [Encyclopedia of Turkish Language and Literature], vol. 6, p. 523.

BIBLIOGRAPHY

ENCYCLOPEDIAS

İslâm Ansiklopedisi, -Komisyon- vol. 9, İstanbul, 1945
Türk Dili Ve Edebiyatı Ansiklopedisi, -Komisyon- vol. 6, İstanbul, 1986
Türkiye Yazarlar Ansiklopedisi, İhsan Işık, Ankara, 2001
Yeni Türk Ansiklopedisi, -Komisyon- vol. 7, İstanbul, 1985

BOOKS

Araz, Nezihe: *Anadolu Erenleri*, İstanbul, 2000
Banarlı, Nihat Sami, *Resimli Türk Edebiyatı Tarihi*, v. 1, İstanbul, 2001
Bayram, Mikâil, *Tarihin Işığında Nasreddin Hoca ve Ahi Evren*, İstanbul, 2001
Boratav, Pertev Nail, *100 Soruda Halk Edebiyatı*, İstanbul, 1969
Cenikoğlu, G. Tarıman; *Akşehir Folklorundan Bir Demet*, Ankara, 2000
Çelebi, Evliya, *Seyahatname*, İstanbul, 1898
Danişmend, İsmail Hami, *Nasreddin Hoca Fıkraları*, İstanbul, 1944
Efe, Ahmet, *Nasreddin Hoca*, İstanbul, 2004
Ergun, Sami, *Manzum Nasreddin Hoca Fıkraları ve Hikâyeleri*, Ankara, 1950
Erkılıç, Cafer, *Evliya Çelebi*, İstanbul, 1969
Eskişehir Valiliği, III. Uluslararası Türk Halk Edebiyatı Semineri Bildir-
    ileri, Eskişehir, 1987
Eyüboğlu, Sabahattin, *Yunus Emre*, İstanbul, 1985
Gölpınarlı, Abdülbaki, *Nasreddin Hoca*, İstanbul, 1961
Güney, Eflatun Cem, *Nasreddin Hoca Fıkraları*, İstanbul, 1974
Kabacalı, Alpay, *Bütün Yönleriyle Nasreddin Hoca*, İstanbul, 2000
Kanık, Orhan Veli, *Nasreddin Hoca Hikayeleri*, İstanbul, 1970
Karahasanoğlu, Sabutay Hikmet, *Nasreddin Hoca*, Ankara, 1991
Konyalı, İbrahim Hakkı, Akşehir, *Nasreddin Hoca'nın Şehri*, İstanbul, 1945
Köprülü, M. Fuad, *Nasreddin Hoca*, Ankara, 2004

Koz, M. Sabri, *Nasreddin Hoca'dan Fıkralar*, İstanbul, 1982

Köseoğlu, Ahmet, *Konya'da Kültür ve Sanat*, Konya, 2004

Kukul, M. Hâlistin, *Şiirlerle Nasreddin Hoca Fıkraları*, Ankara, 1989

Kurdakul, Şükran, *Şair ve Yazarlar Sözlüğü*, İstanbul, 1989

Kurgan, Şükrü, *Nasreddin Hoca*, Ankara, 1986

Kültür Bakanlığı, Uluslararası 1. Nasreddin Hoca Sempozyumu Bildirileri, Ankara, 1990

Kültür Bakanlığı, *Nasreddin Hoca Seksiyon Bildirileri*, Ankara, 1996

Lâmizade Abdullah Çelebi, *Letaif*, Hz. Yaşar Çalışkan, İstanbul, 1978

Necatigil, Behçet, *Edebiyatımızda İsimler Sözlüğü*, İstanbul, 1975

Özbek, Abdullah, *Bir Eğitimci Olarak Nasreddin Hoca*, Konya, 2004

Sakaoğlu, Saim, *Türk Fıkraları ve Nasreddin Hoca*, Konya, 1992

Tokmakçıoğlu, Erdoğan, *Bütün Yönleriyle Nasreddin Hoca*, İstanbul, 1971

Türkmen, Fikret, *Letaif-i Nasreddin Hoca*, Burhaniye Tercümesi, Ankara, 1989

Uçman, Duhter, *Nasreddin Hoca ile Çocuklar*, İstanbul, 1993

Uzun, Kemal, *Nasreddin Hoca Araştırması*, İstanbul, 1988

Yakupoğlu, Ahmet, *Minyatürlerle Nasreddin Hoca Fıkraları*, İstanbul, 1999

JOURNALS

Türk Dili dergisi, Türk Halk Edebiyatı Özel Sayısı, Issue 207, Ankara, 1968

Türk Edebiyatı, Nasreddin Hoca Anıt Sayısı, Issue 255, İstanbul, 1995

Yedi İklim dergisi, Nasreddin Hoca Özel Sayısı. Issue 138–139, İstanbul, 2001

INDEX